HOUSEHOLDER'S ACTION GUIDE

a Consumer Publication

Consumers' Association
publishers of **Which?**
14 Buckingham Street
London WC2N6DS

a Consumer Publication

edited by   Edith Rudinger

illustrations by   Malcolm Hollis
on whose draft text
this book is based

published by   Consumers' Association
publishers of **Which?**

Consumer publications
are available from
Consumers' Association
and from booksellers.

© Consumers' Association October 1984

ISBN 0 85202 284 9
and   0 340 36089 5

Photoset by Paston Press, Norwich
Printed in Great Britain by
Richard Clay (The Chaucer Press) Ltd,
Bungay, Suffolk

contents

Neighbours   5
Trees   16
Nuisance   23
Neighbour's building work   34
Landlord, repairs and eviction   42
Maintenance, defects and remedies   50
Calling in expert help   65
Employing a builder   70
Claiming on insurance   81
The local authority   86
Getting a grant   96
Building Regulations approval   105
Planning permission   113
Rates   128
Which? reports   138
Index   140

neighbours

Neighbours have rights and obligations to each other, and some shared responsibilities.

In taking up any matter which involves a neighbour, bear in mind that you will be living opposite or alongside each other for many years to come, and will want to enjoy a reasonably happy relationship. So, in the first place, try to talk things over and try to sort out problems in an amicable fashion before taking action, and use tact or diplomacy whenever you can.

party walls

Where two properties are joined and share what is commonly called a party wall, there is usually a right of support. Such a right almost certainly exists if the properties are over 20 years old and the wall has been shared over that period.

The owners of the properties must not do anything which would damage the structural support of the party wall; any building works the adjoining owner carries out to his property must not damage the walls which are common to the two properties. In an extreme situation, if the next-door property is going to be demolished, the owner of that property would have to ensure that the party wall is adequately supported and will not be damaged.

If anything you do to your property damages the adjoining building, you may have to compensate the neighbour for any financial loss which he has suffered as a result, and vice versa.

work that affects neighbour's property

If your property is a terraced house, or is in some way connected to your neighbour's, you should notify him if any building works you propose to carry out will in any way affect the walls shared by both buildings.

Where there is no specific information to the contrary, the boundary is assumed to run through the centre of the wall and each half may be dealt with independently by the two owners. If you wish to extend the party wall and the adjoining owner does not, you can raise your half-wall, provided you do not damage his half of the building or his half of the wall.

party wall agreement

You may reach a party wall agreement with the adjoining owner that you may carry out proposals that affect the structure which separates the two dwellings. There may be an agreement regarding the hours during which work may be carried out, so that the banging and noise does not unreasonably interfere with the adjoining owner's use of the property.

Party wall agreements usually contain a schedule of the condition of the adjoining owner's premises prior to the building work.

Many people notice cracks which have been there for years only after builders set to work on the other side of the wall. Having a schedule before work begins may prevent long and involved arguments over the age of the crack, who caused it, and who is going to pay for it to be repaired. It is the neighbour who is going to have the work carried out who pays for preparing the schedule.

Inner London

In London, the rules about party walls are slightly different: the broad principle is that a party wall is owned in common, with each person having the right to carry out work, provided no damage is caused to the other person's property or the wall itself altered.

Two months' notice of the intention to carry out work must be given to the adjoining owner if it will affect the party wall. Works for which notice must be given includes any cutting into it to impose an extra load or for chases for electrical work, raising the party wall if you are going to build an extra floor on your building, or the redistribution of loading within the property where partitions which butt against the party wall are to be removed.

Where the property on the other side of the party wall is in multiple occupation, notice must be served on every occupant or owner. So, for a building in the middle of a terrace, with two large apartment houses on each side, it may mean serving twenty or thirty notices.

if you proceed without consent
If building work is started without the approval of the adjoining owner, he may demand service of a notice for the work to stop within two months. He would be able to obtain an injunction to prevent work being carried out until the documentation was complete.

There is a provision for a fine to be levied on a day-to-day basis for not having submitted the relevant notices. This fine is levied by the district surveyor, but does not recompense the neighbour who has suffered as a result of the building work being carried out.

neighbour's disrepair

The duty of care which neighbours owe each other as owners of adjoining properties extends to taking reasonable steps to prevent damage being caused to each other's building.

If your neighbour has failed to repair his property, and the damage has caused the support or structure of your building to deteriorate, you are entitled to take the necessary steps to make sure that your building does not suffer further. This includes going into his property yourself and carrying out repairs to part of the building.

But if you want to get the adjoining owner to carry out the

necessary work at his expense, you would have to take him to court on the basis of his negligence. You would have to prove that the adjoining owner was aware of the problems and the likely damage to your property, and did nothing about it.

For example, where a neighbour's building has been left with badly damaged guttering or downpipes which allow a wall to become very wet, a claim for damages caused through the neighbour's negligence may succeed.

But there is no point seeking a remedy through the courts in an isolated instance, such as a pipe leak or a broken rainwater pipe which is repaired. This is better dealt with by making an insurance claim.

Even if the damaged pipe is your neighbour's, your own insurance should pay under the 'escape of water' clause. Your insurers would then subrogate on your neighbour's to get their money back, because he caused the damage. Or, if your neighbour has liability insurance, provided that he was actually liable at law, that would pay. You cannot claim on your neighbour's policy, but it may well be worth asking your neighbour to pass the matter to his insurers.

house being pulled down

If you are aware that the house adjoining yours is to be demolished, contact the local authority and ask them to serve a notice on your neighbour (under section 27 of the Public Health Act 1961) irrespective of whether demolition has already begun or the neighbouring owner only intends to demolish.

This notice requires the person on whom it is served to:

* shore up any building adjacent to the one to which the notice relates
* weatherproof any surfaces of adjacent building which are exposed by the demolition
* repair and make good any damage caused by the demolition or by the negligent act or omission of any person engaged in it.

boundaries

The boundary of a property, irrespective of whether it is a flat, a house, a garden, an allotment or an estate, is ultimately a fine line, drawn on a map or plan. That fine line may be difficult to locate.

where exactly is the boundary?

Where there is a dispute between adjoining property owners about the precise location of a boundary, they should first check the plans or other documentation.

Attached to the title deeds, lease, or land certificate, is usually a plan on which are shown the boundaries of the land over which you have control. In some documents, the boundaries are nicely coloured and marked with a red line. In others, there is a written reference to the location of boundaries – which may, however, be complicated and open to various interpretations.

Sometimes the plan will indicate boundaries in one area and the written words suggest that they should be somewhere different.

In disputes, the indication on the plan would prevail over written words, but if the plan is marked as 'for identification only', clear words prevail.

The Land Registry filed plan indicates general boundaries only and cannot be used in boundary disputes, unless noted as fixed, in which case it prevails. But the registrar has power to determine disputes.

Where a line on a plan indicates a boundary between two properties, it is common practice to show a T-mark on one side of the line. This means that the particular fence or hedge belongs to the owner of the property inside which the T-mark appears. But for conclusive evidence, the plan has to be backed by a reference in the deeds relating to the presence of the T-marks.

some presumptions about boundaries

If there is no definite evidence as to
location and ownership of a boundary,
certain presumptions apply.

If there is a ditch and then a hedge or
bank, you own the land up to the ditch,
because it is presumed that a person
cannot cut a ditch in another man's
land). This applies only where it is a
single, man-made, ditch. If an ordnance
map is used to describe the property in
the deeds, the boundary line is the centre
of the ditch.

Similarly, if a piece of land appears to
terminate with a hedge beyond which is
a ditch, the presumption is that the
boundary lies on the edge of the ditch
which is farther from the bank or hedge.
This assumption is based on the premise
that the originator of the ditch stood on
the edge of his own land, and throwing
the soil further onto his land, the bank
which then was formed was used as the
base of the hedge.

If the boundary to a garden or a piece of land is a private right of
way, the line of the boundary is presumed to be the centre line of
the right of way.

Where the boundary seems to be in the form of a hedge, if either
of the parties has over the years been responsible for trimming the
hedge, it is possible that he may be able to rely on the presumption
that the boundary lies on the outer edge of the hedge over which this
act of ownership was exercised.

acquiring a right

If a land owner takes possession of land beyond his boundary and keeps that possession undisputed and without acknowledgment of the true owner's title to it, for twelve years or more, it is most likely that the law will accept that he has become the owner of it – by what is known as adverse possession. After that period of twelve years, the former owner cannot take court action to recover it.

rivers and lakes

Where a non-tidal river or other natural stream or water course forms the boundary, the boundary line is presumed to be the middle of the stream. If natural small changes take place in the alignment of the river, the boundary will change with them. Where the changes have been made deliberately – perhaps the river has been redirected – the line of the boundary will be along the centre of the former bed of the stream or river.

If there is an island in the middle of the stream, the boundary will run in the centre of the section of water between your land and the island.

None of these presumptions apply for artificial water courses, such as a canal or man-made ditch. There is also no presumption as to the location of the boundary where the edge of your property is at a lake or pond.

rights over the use of water

If the boundary of your land joins a natural stream or lake (not artificial waters, such as reservoirs, canals, or ponds), you will in normal circumstances have certain rights over the water, such as the right to fish in it.

You have a right to pass over the water between the edge of your land and the boundary, by swimming, or in a boat. If you have a boat, you can load and unload it, but you would not necessarily have a right to moor it, or beach it, unless in so doing you draw it off the surface of the water and onto your dry land, so that you do not impede the passage of water or the movement of other people over the water.

fences, hedges, boundary walls

Even if there is no argument about the exact boundary, there may be with regard to the ownership of a particular fence, or wall, and responsibility for its repair or maintenance.

The title documents may indicate responsibility for upkeep of a boundary fence or wall. If not, common sense may have to prevail, or – for the sake of living in peace with neighbours – a compromise reached.

There is a popular belief, but no legal basis for the presumption, that a wooden fence inevitably belongs to the owner of the land on the side where the supporting posts are. If the fence is maintained by the owner of one of the adjoining properties, there is a presumption that he owns the fence. Otherwise, the fence may be declared a 'party fence' (similar to a party wall), notionally divided vertically down the middle with both owners having rights of support but no obligation to maintain it. But if any repair work is carried out, both owners must contribute to the cost.

mending your fences

If the boundary fence is falling down, the person who owns that fence does not have to replace or repair it unless it constitutes a danger in its present state, with the risk of injuring a neighbour if it were to collapse.

If a fence needs repairing and you have to go onto your neighbour's land to carry out the repairs, you have to ask his permission. The law does not give any general right of entry for repair, even if it is the only practical means of doing this job. If you do go onto his land without permission, your neighbour could take you to court in a civil action for trespass.

prescriptive right

However, there are certain circumstances where a right of entry can be established. This is if, for a period of at least twenty years, the occupiers of the land have, from time to time, gone onto the neighbour's land without permission to carry out work on the fence or wall, whenever necessary, and the neighbour has never objected to this action, nor charged a fee for it. This is called a right of prescription.

Where you have recently bought your property and realise that the only possible and practical way of maintaining the boundary is via your neighbour's property, and you know that it has been the practice of the previous owners of your property to do so, the prescriptive right to enter becomes yours, as the new owner.

Prescriptive rights of entry are rarely set down in black and white and generally depend on people's personal recollections. Therefore, in a dispute, it only needs the neighbour to say that on each occasion his permission was sought, for the prescriptive right not to exist. All that would be needed is "Excuse me, I hope you don't mind if I trim my hedge": such words would be seeking permission, and the prescriptive right would be lost.

If the fence, hedge or wall has been set back from the boundary line so as to retain a strip of land beyond the boundary for repair, maintenance, trimming of hedges, the actual location of the boundary may disappear in time. If the adjoining landowner then uses that strip as his land for a period of over twenty years, he may acquire a prescriptive right to it.

no fences

In most cases, unless there is an agreement which is binding on either or both parties, there is no requirement to mark the boundary of your land, nor to enclose it.

On some housing estates built this century, the title deeds of the property contain restrictive covenants forbidding fences or boundaries being placed to the front of properties, so that the estate will maintain its uniform layout and appearance. Where such covenants outlive their usefulness, it is possible to make an application for them to be set aside. You would, however, have to be able to substantiate that the covenant has become totally worthless, or unworkable or inconsistent.

A building lease (where land is sold for a period of, say, 99 years, and the person who buys it then builds on it) may require the provision of a fence of a particular type or design. Someone who has just bought a house in some suburban location with a sixty year lease may not realise that it was originally a building lease unless he carefully reads the documentation.

Planning legislation controls the height of boundary fences. The maximum height for a front fence along street boundaries is one metre and for a rear fence 2 metres. Should you wish to erect a higher fence you would need to apply for planning permission.

trimming the hedge

Where the boundary is a hedge, it is assumed that, unless there is evidence to the contrary, the boundary line runs through the centre of the hedge.
Problems may then arise concerning the clipping and control of the growth of the hedge: if one side wants to let more sun into the garden, and would like to reduce the height of the hedge, the adjoining owner may not agree.

If the hedge is the boundary, the property owners are jointly responsible for it, which means that neither can do anything to it which would reduce it in size or injure it, without the agreement of the other.

The hedge may be the visual barrier between the two properties, but if the documentation shows that it actually grows on the land of one or the other of the neighbouring property owners, it is entirely within the control of the person who owns the land it grows on. He may reduce its height or encourage its growth or chop it into interesting shapes. The adjoining property owner will only be able to control the growth from spreading onto his property and must not do anything that would damage the hedge.

He should notify the neighbour that he wishes to trim the branches which overhang his property (and, strictly speaking, once the branches are cut off they belong to the next-door neighbour). In theory, he should offer them to him or place them on the neighbour's side of the boundary.

trees

If a tree is at a boundary between properties, it may be difficult to establish whose it is and who is responsible for it, unless the deeds, the lease, or the plans at the Land Registry, show a boundary clearly and unequivocally. If there is no evidence to the contrary, some presumptions apply.

The tree belongs to the owner of the land in which it was originally planted; this applies even if the tree roots have spread across the line of the boundary and now run under the adjoining land, or its branches are beyond the line of the boundary.

It is a popular misconception that a tree on a boundary line belongs to the property over which its branch spread predominates.

Ownership is determined by where the tree trunk is in relation to the boundary. The position and extent of the roots and branches do not have any influence on ownership, only the trunk does. If, say, two-thirds of the trunk is over the boundary into one property and one-third to the other, the tree is the responsibility of the owners in the proportions of 3:2 even if the tree was all on one side of the boundary when smaller.

If the exact location of the boundary is in doubt, evidence of careful husbandry by one party who has maintained and trimmed the tree, may give him rights over, and responsibilities for, it by virtue of his husbandry.

trouble with roots

The roots of most trees spread at least as far as the branches overhang the ground, so it is likely that tree roots on, or near, a boundary will have spread into adjoining land. A tree owner is not obliged to prevent the roots of his tree from spreading into a neighbouring garden. The neighbour has every right to cut off roots which spread onto his land, but if the tree suffers as a result, he could be liable for damages.

Tree roots can cause damage to property by varying or reducing the moisture content of clay soil, and affecting the foundations of a property. Minor roots may damage or block drains if they are already leaking, because water will attract the roots.

If tree roots cause, or contribute to, actual damage, the owner of the tree may be liable. But it would be up to you to prove that the damage has been caused by the tree roots, and to show which tree is responsible.

There are specialist consultants (for example, Botanical Identification, 49 Whiteknights Road, Reading RG6 2BB) who identify tree root samples, for a fee. Root samples are usually sent on behalf of insurance companies, but there is no reason why you should not do this yourself, if you are involved in such a dispute. You may need a surveyor's report to show that damage to your house was caused by the neighbour's tree.

If you suspect that a neighbour's tree is damaging the foundations of your house (which is likely only on clay soil) , you should contact your neighbour and your insurance company immediately.

Your buildings insurance covers damage to your house by your neighbour's tree being uprooted in a storm, or if your neighbour's tree falls on it for whatever cause (not only storm), because the cover would be under the 'impact' section of the policy. But if the roots of his tree undermine the foundations of your house, your insurance does not normally give you cover for this: his insurance should pay for it, provided he has a legal obligation to compensate you.

The owner of a healthy, properly maintained tree is unlikely to be liable for damage done to a neighbour's property if the tree, or some of its branches, fall as a result of unforeseen and exceptional weather conditions – lightning or a gale, for example. But if the tree owner has been negligent and the tree or its branches fall as a result of decay or disease, or damage that he knew about, he would be liable for any damage caused.

overhanging branches

If your neighbour's tree overhangs your boundary, he is not obliged to remove the overhanging branches unless they cause actual damage, or a court orders him to do so. But you can cut them off – or have them cut off, at your expense – provided you do not go beyond the boundary line. You do not have to consult him first, but it would be polite to do so. The branches you cut still belong to him, so you must offer to return them. He does not have to accept them, but you must not simply dump them on his land.

You may not pick fruit from a branch overhanging your garden, without the neighbour's permission, because it belongs to him, and so does any fruit which falls on to your land from his fruit tree.

If a tree merely obstructs your light and its branches do not actually overhang your property, you probably cannot make the tree owner do anything about it if he does not want to (unless there is a prescriptive right of light – that is, one acquired through uninterrupted use over twenty years).

anticipating problems

People who plant a tree should bear in mind its likely size twenty or even fifty years on. One way of avoiding problems with trees is to select the species wisely.

You should keep a regular check on your trees for any problems which you may be able to deal with, such as disease, and prevent overgrowing by a careful programme of pruning.

A professional arboriculturist (or tree care specialist, sometimes still called a 'tree surgeon') can give specialist advice on problems with trees. If you employ a specialist on your property, you may be held responsible if he causes damage – for example, if a large branch falls on someone's car. Make sure he has public liability insurance cover (advisable minimum: £250,000). Some contractors do not have insurance and just walk off when there is an accident. You should check the address of the firm and the insurance cover before the work starts.

The Arboricultural Association (Ampfield House, Ampfield, near Romsey, Hants, SO5 9PA), has a free list of approved contractors and consultants, area by area. You can also get advice from the Royal Forestry Society (102 High Street, Tring, Herts, HP23 4AH). Many local authorities have lists of tree consultants and contractors in their area. The Forestry Commission Research Station, Alice Holt Lodge, near Farnham, Surrey (telephone: 0420 22255) will offer advice by letter and telephone, but will not visit the site.

trees in the street

Most trees in the street belong to the local authority or, perhaps, following a road widening scheme, a tree may belong to an adjacent property owner.

If you suspect that a tree might be dangerous, notify the council in writing of the location of the tree, and ask them to make it safe. Irrespective of whose tree it is, the local authority is empowered to take any action they feel appropriate, depending on the condition of the tree; this would include felling it.

If you think tree roots are causing damage to your foundations, it is up to you to prove it – the local authority will not investigate the problem for you. You may need to have the tree roots identified and need a report from a specialist consultant and a surveyor.

If a tree on the pavement outside your house is depriving you of light, complain to the local authority who may thin out the tree to allow more light to come through. You are entitled to prune any branches which overhang your boundary.

unsafe trees

If there is a dangerous tree in your own garden, which might cause damage or injury to passers-by and you do nothing about it, or such a tree is in a property you once owned and have now left, or in your neighbour's garden, or in the street, anyone who believes that it may be dangerous, can notify the council of the tree and its location.

The council may try and trace the owners of the land on which the tree is situated and will give them 21 days to take such action as may be necessary to make the tree safe. A person receiving such notice may appeal on one of the following grounds:

* that he is neither the owner nor the occupier of the land on which the tree stands
* that the tree is not in a dangerous condition
* that the tree can be made safe more cheaply than the manner the notice proposes
* that the notice should have been served on the occupier of the land (if you are the owner), and that he is the person who is responsible. (In the case of certain tenancies, the owner of the land rather than the occupier is responsible for trees.)

The council may themselves take steps to make a tree safe, if there is an imminent risk of damage and they cannot trace the owner or the occupier.

British Standards 3998, *Recommendations for Tree Work (1966)* lays down procedures for all aspects of tree surgery. If the local authority specifies the work to be done to a tree – either because it is protected or because they consider it to be dangerous – they will not compel you to employ a tree consultant but they will require the British Standard to be followed.

poisonous trees

If you have a poisonous tree, such as a laburnum, near your boundary and you allow the branches to overhang your neighbour's property, you might be liable if your neighbour's children or animals eat the seeds, leaves or berries and are poisoned.

If you spray your tree with a poisonous chemical and it drifts into your neighbour's property, causing damage to crops, animals or people, you could be lible for the damage.

tree preservation

The local planning authority have powers to protect trees by making a preservation order, with regard to single trees, groups of trees or woodland (but not hedges, bushes or shrubs). If a protected tree is cut down, uprooted or wilfully destroyed or damaged, or topped or lopped in a way that might destroy it, the person responsible may be fined up to £1,000 in the magistrates court, or twice the value of the tree if that is more.

taking action

A tree preservation order is made generally, but not exclusively, where trees are immediately at risk of being felled, destroyed or damaged. If there are any trees in your neighbourhood which you think should be protected, give details of them, including a location map, to the local planning authority and put forward your reasons why you believe a preservation order should be made.

An owner on whom a notice is served can object (within 28 days of the notice), and indeed anyone may make representations to the local planning authority for or against an order.

after an order

When an order has been made, the local authority does not take over responsibility for looking after the trees, but the owner has to get the authority's consent before undertaking any lopping or felling. The exceptions to this include cutting down a dead or dangerous tree, or where it is necessary to cut down a tree in order to prevent a nuisance which would be actionable in law.

But even where consent is not required, at least five days' notice has to be given of the proposal to cut down a protected tree that is dead or dangerous and, unless the authority agrees otherwise, the tree has to be replaced. The new tree is protected by the original preservation order.

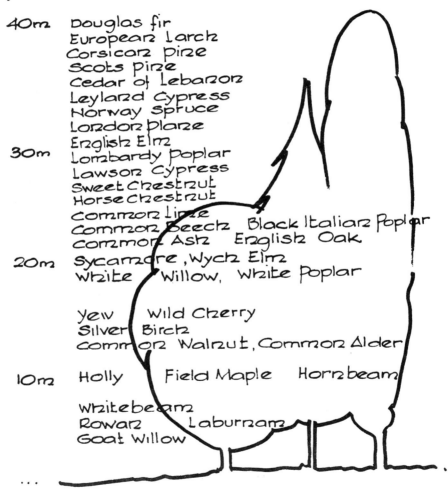

40m Douglas fir
European Larch
Corsican pine
Scots pine
Cedar of Lebanon
Leyland Cypress
Norway spruce
London plane
English Elm

30m Lombardy poplar
Lawson Cypress
Sweet Chestnut
Horse Chestnut
common Lime
common Beech   Black Italian Poplar
common Ash   English Oak

20m Sycamore, Wych Elm
white   Willow, White Poplar

Yew   Wild Cherry
Silver Birch
common Walnut, Common Alder

10m Holly   Field Maple   Hornbeam

Whitebeam
Rowan   Laburnam
Goat Willow

AVERAGE HEIGHT OF TREES

nuisance

Everybody has their own interpretation of the word nuisance with regard to neighbours: it may be irritation caused by the neighbour's children throwing balls into your garden, smoke drifting over from a summer bonfire, the noise of a family row. These annoyances are not, strictly speaking, nuisance. Nuisance (private, public or statutory) has a special meaning in law.

Acts of parliament such as the Clean Air Acts, the Control of Pollution Act, Public Health Acts can declare certain actions or omissions a nuisance, so that an individual can bring a complaint. Local by-laws can give the local authority power to take action, or issue a notice demanding action, where some particular circumstances cause discomfort or annoyance.

Noise or vibration can amount to a nuisance. Smoke other than that emitted from chimneys or from industrial premises may constitute a nuisance if it causes annoyance to the neighbourhood, and the local authority is empowered to act.

For a 'public' nuisance, it must be shown that the annoyance is a result of something done or left undone which has materially affected the comfort and quality of life for the people in the neighbourhood, or caused an interference for a substantial period of time. A 'private' nuisance is caused by unreasonable interference with the use or enjoyment of one's own property.

nuisance and neighbours

Between neighbours, a nuisance may be caused by one person doing on his own land something which he is lawfully entitled to do, but this becomes a nuisance when whatever he is doing causes damage to his neighbour's land, or encroaches beyond his boundaries, or causes some interference.

is a bonfire reasonable, or a nuisance?

In many cases, the cause and the effect will be a matter of fact and what is at issue is whether the event or activity on a neighbour's land was reasonable or not. Lighting a bonfire to burn some waste on your own land is a perfectly legitimate activity: to light one every day may be an inconvenience – but whether it is actually a nuisance depends on the level of inconvenience that your neighbour suffers, and the extent to which it has interfered with his enjoyment of his land, garden, property or buildings.

If you repeatedly have smoky bonfires which annoy the neighbours, your local authority, if they think that the nuisance is likely to continue, can apply to the magistrates' court for a 'nuisance order' (under s. 16 of the Clean Air Act 1956) to prevent you from having further bonfires. It is an offence to cause a nuisance through the creation of smoke; the maximum penalty is £500.

What is more, an individual, such as the neighbour, can complain directly to the magistrates if he can show what nuisance the bonfires caused, state when they were lit, and give details of who else has been affected.

A leaflet published by the National Society for Clean Air gives the following advice on how to prevent a smoke nuisance:

> ● **Compost** as much garden rubbish as possible. Some local councils will collect bagged garden rubbish with the household waste; some will take it away for a small charge; others permit garden rubbish to be dumped at the municipal depot. Check how your authority can help you.

- **If you must light** a fire, ensure that only dry material is burnt. This will produce the minimum of smoke. Never add household rubbish or rubber tyres to the fire, or use sump oil to set it alight.
- **Do not light** a fire when weather conditions will cause problems. Smoke hangs in the air on damp, windless days and in the evening around sunset.
- **Don't burn** when the wind will carry smoke over other people's property, or over roads.
- **Bonfires can be dangerous,** and should never be left unattended. Don't leave a fire to smoulder – douse it with soil or water.

Moreover, burning things on one's own ground could cause damage if the fire got out of hand; if it damages trees in the adjoining garden or the boundary fence, it will constitute a nuisance and be your responsibility.

trespass

A trespasser is a person who enters another's land without permission. The practical remedy is to ask him to leave. If he does not, you are entitled to use sufficient force – but not more – to eject him. You are not entitled to assault or harm a trespasser in any way.

Responsibility to a trespasser extends to taking steps to prevent circumstances which may endanger him. The greater the likelihood of trespassers, the more precautions should be taken. For example, where property is being altered or demolished, it is possible that the land may become a playground for young children after the builders have left in the evening. You owe a duty of care to those children to ensure that they will not be injured even though they are trespassers.

If your pet dog bites a trespasser, you are unlikely to be liable for the injury this causes. However, if you keep a fierce Dobermann Pinscher solely for the protection of your property, you could be liable for injuries it causes.

The police will rarely interfere in cases of trespass because this is a civil matter and not a criminal one. So, putting up a notice stating 'trespassers will be prosecuted' is likely to be an empty threat, unless the trespasser on your property is carrying an offensive weapon.

trespass against property

When somebody places something on your land without your permission, this is a trespass even if it is only somebody fixing something to the wall of your house. (Moreover, fly-posting requires planning permission – in theory. In practice, it is generally impossible to find out the name of the person or company actually putting up the advertisements or posters and without this information there is nothing the local authority can do about it.)

If creepers or other plants are growing on the face of your wall, from roots in your neighbour's property, this is also a trespass. You could take action if this creeper is likely to cause damage to the wall of your property, and you are entitled to cut it off.

Your neighbour propping a ladder up against your wall would be trespass. It is reasonable to request that he removes it if it is likely to cause damage. In all cases where neighbours are involved, try to deal with any matters of dispute in a reasonable manner rather than resort to an action in law.

other nuisance

Damage may, for example, be caused by a gutter overflowing and discharging water over the neighbour's property, or mounds of earth placed against the wall of an adjoining house bridging the damp proof course and letting damp get into the building.

The use of toxic substances, such as spraying plants in your window boxes with weed killer, is your own business. But in a high wind, if the spray is blown on to other properties, damage will be your responsibility.

neighbours' children and stray balls

Children playing football in the back garden will sooner or later send the ball into a neighbouring garden.

If you find a ball in the middle of your lawn, you must not get rid of it. Using it to play with, or disposing of it, would be legal 'conversion'. If the owner asks for it, you must give the ball back to him, but you do not have to try and find the owner.

If you or your children throw a ball on your neighbour's land, you do not have the right to enter and reclaim it. So ask politely "May we have our ball back, please?".

Where your property overlooks a golf course, cricket or recreational ground, or other areas where balls are flying about, make sure that you are adequately covered by insurance for the eventuality of damage they may cause.

In general, responsibility for damage caused by golf balls hit from a golf course, or cricket balls from a cricket ground, or hockey balls from a sports field, is the owner's of the ground from which the damage has been caused. But it may be difficult to prove negligence, and expensive to substantiate it, especially if the club has taken all proper precautions.

A person who strikes a golf ball from a golf course directly at the plate glass windows of an adjoining property, with a deliberate intent to cause damage, is responsible for the consequences of his actions. A golfer who is attempting to blast his way out of a bunker, and who mishits the ball, so that it disappears in a wholly unintended direction, will have caused damage by accident and not by intent.

insurance

Provided that your house is occupied, you will have insurance cover for accidental breakage of fixed glass, but that is all – unless you have one of the more expensive all-risks policies. There is a small amount of cover under your contents policy, if the glass tops of your furniture or your television set was damaged by the ball, but again, that is all.

What you really need to know is whether the person who hit the ball has personal liability insurance (perhaps under a block policy for the club, or as part of one of the various sportsman's insurances that a private player can have). If so, make a claim on him because his insurance company will pay.

animals

If an animal has caused damage to you or your property, you may be able to sue the person who was responsible for that animal, in the civil courts under the law of negligence. He would be liable only if you could show that he had a duty to take reasonbable care of the animal and failed in that duty, and that the injury or damage resulted from this.

Irrespective of any negligence, there is a general liability for the control of animals. If the person responsible for looking after the animal knows that it is likely to cause damage if not adequately restrained, or that the animal is particularly vicious, he is liable for all damage which is caused.

There are exceptions:

- if the damage was the fault of the person who was injured because he took stupid risks with the animal – such as teasing a dog; or if the person who was injured knew of the risk of injury but ignored it
- if the person who is injured is a trespasser (unless it was unreasonable to keep such an animal)
- cats.

A police officer can detain a dog which has been worrying livestock. If you own a dog which attacks or chases livestock on agricultural land, you will be liable to a fine. If your dog kills or injures livestock, you will be liable for the damage, unless the livestock has strayed on to your land.

If two or more dogs together cause any damage or injury, each will be treated as being the cause of the whole damage, and both or all the owners of the dogs held responsible.

The owner of any animal which has an infectious or contagious disease is liable for any damage that may be caused as a result, provided he knew that the animal was infected.

animals and fencing

There is a specific obligation to provide substantial fences if you keep dangerous animals, to prevent them escaping.

If your property is inadequately fenced between the road and the edge of your garden and an animal gets on to your land, it is unlikely that you will be successful in being recompensed for any damage it does. For that, it would be necessary to prove negligence against the person responsible for the animal.

noise from neighbours

If you have noisy neighbours, tell them that they are disturbing you – they may not be aware of it. And tell them what, in particular, is causing trouble: loud music, animals, plumbing. Have an informal discussion with them to see if you can reach an amicable agreement. Remember any noise you yourself cause might equally disturb them, or others.

If this has no effect, and you still suffer from the noise, three courses of action are open to you:

* complaint to the local authority
* complaint direct to magistrates' court (in Scotland, summary application to the sheriff court)
* civil action – that is, taking the neighbour to court yourself.

complaint to local authority

This is often the most satisfactory way of dealing with a noise nuisance. Section 58 of the Control of Pollution Act 1974 gives local authorities powers to deal with noise from a house, factory, garden or open ground which they consider amounts to a statutory nuisance.

Explain the problem to the environmental health department of your local authority. An officer from the department will normally carry out a preliminary investigation and discuss the matter with you. He must make a judgment on the crucial point of whether the noise amounts to a statutory nuisance: he cannot just take the word of the complainant.

Noise is a subjective thing, and different people react to it in different ways. What causes extreme annoyance to one person may be hardly noticed by another. A noise, however irritating, may not necessarily be a nuisance in the legal sense. In deciding whether a noise is sufficient to amount to a nuisance, the environmental health officer has to consider what would be the likely reaction of the average, reasonable person to the noise, taking into account not only its volume, but also such factors as when, how often and for how long the noise occurs.

This is generally simpler when the noise is, for example, amplified music. Complaints about noises of ordinary living, or where noise is due to lack of soundproofing, are more tricky because it is up to individuals how they live their lives and difficult to restrict, for example, shouting, or loud quarrelling.

Many complaints relate to noise late at night or weekends. Although local authorities will normally try to be helpful, they are limited in staff but you can try ringing the local authority number if you are subjected to excessive noise late at night. This might result in a security patrol being sent out to deal with the noise.

If the local authority is satisfied that the noise constitutes a nuisance, they usually contact the person who is responsible and attempt to resolve the matter informally. If this fails, they may serve a notice on the person causing the noise, or on the owner or occupier of the premises. (But they will serve a notice only after they have heard the noise for themselves.)

The notice will 'require the abatement of the nuisance' – that is, stopping the noise, and it may specify how this is to be achieved. If the recipient does not comply with the notice, proceedings can be taken against him in the magistrates' court (in Scotland, in the sheriff court). The local authority can also seek an injunction (in the High Court, and in Scotland it may seek interdict in the Court of Session or sheriff court) but does so only exceptionally for a dispute between neighbours. An injunction is a court order telling a person what he must do, or stop doing. If he does not comply, he is in contempt of court and could be sent to prison.

If the noise was caused in the course of a trade or business (not by a private person in domestic circumstances), the person who caused it has a defence if he can prove that he has done his practical best to prevent or counteract the effect of the noise. This recognises that there is a limit to what it is reasonable to require a person to do, or to spend, in order to reduce noise, and that there may be technical limitations.

complaint direct to magistrates

You yourself can complain directly to the magistrates' court under section 59 of the Control of Pollution Act 1974. Again, the magistrates will need to be persuaded that the noise amounts to a nuisance. It can help establish the case if you have kept a written record of the dates, times and duration of the noise, the type of noise (loud music, banging, whatever), and of any action taken by you, such as requests to be quiet, and can produce it in the court.

Before making an official complaint, try to resolve the problem informally by writing to the person responsible for the noise (the local authority will do this for you, too, if you ask for their help), or to the owner or occupier of the premises. Say that you consider he is making a noise amounting to a nuisance, and unless he stops or satisfactorily reduces the noise, you feel that you will have little choice but to take your complaint to the magistrates' court. Date the letter and keep a copy, because it will help if you can show that you have acted in a reasonable manner, and have given those responsible the chance to resolve the situation before you resorted to legal measures.

If you do need to make a formal complaint, contact the clerk of the court and tell him you wish to make a complaint under section 59 of the Control of Pollution Act 1974. You do not have to pay a court fee.

You will be told on what day you have to come back to court and appear as a witness. If the court agrees, it will make an order that the neighbour must 'abate the nuisance'; if he does not comply, he can be brought back to court and can be fined. If the neighbour is found guilty, a fine of up to £200 can be imposed (up to £400 for a subsequent similar offence). This in itself may not stop the noise, but a fine of £50 a day can be imposed for each day on which the offence continues after conviction.

summary application to the sheriff (in Scotland)

In Scotland, you have to make a summary application to the sheriff for an order to abate the nuisance or to prohibit or restrict its occurrence. It may be advisable to take legal advice before proceeding this far. The sheriff clerk will give you a warrant fixing a date for the case to call in court. A copy of the application and warrant will be served on the person responsible for the noise (if you have no solicitor, you will have to arrange for a sheriff officer or solicitor to do this on your behalf). If the application is not defended, the sheriff may proceed to make whatever order he thinks fit in the circumstances; if it is defended, a date will be fixed for hearing evidence.

civil action

You can take civil action yourself and seek an injunction to restrain the neighbour from continuing the nuisance (and possibly claim damages). But in order to succeed, you must be able to show that the noise causes inconvenience beyond what other occupiers in the neighbourhood can be expected to bear.

Civil action can be very expensive and it is advisable first to seek advice from a citizens' advice bureau or a solicitor.

the police
If you complain about noise to the police, they may be sympathetic but cannot do anything about it, even if an all-night disco party keeps you, and the whole neighbourhood, awake.

complaints about traffic noise

You should address complaints or suggestions about the routeing or regulation of traffic to your local traffic authority which, in England and Wales, is your county or district council (in Scotland, the regional or islands council). Although authorities welcome constructive ideas, they may not be able to take positive action.

compensation for depreciation in property value

You may be able to claim compensation from whoever caused the noise if the value of your property depreciates by more than £50 as a result of noise (and other physical factors) arising from, for example, new or substantially altered roads, and airports. A booklet explaining how the scheme works, *Your home and nuisance from public development* (no. 2 in the series on the Land Compensation Code: *Land Compensation – your rights explained*), can be obtained free from local council offices or citizens' advice bureaux.

Even if you do not qualify, it may be worth checking with your valuation officer to see whether you can obtain a rate reduction because of the increased noise.

Free booklets issued by the Department of the Environment and the Scottish Office explain the regulations about the insulation of dwellings against construction and traffic noise arising from new or improved roads, and how an occupier can find out whether his dwelling qualifies for a grant. *Insulation against traffic noise* (no. 5 in the series about the Land Compensation Code) can be obtained from local council offices and citizens' advice bureaux.

neighbour's building work

Neighbours, however close geographically, are sometimes in that awkward relationship to each other which is neither family and friends nor strangers or enemies. Because of this, there may be lack of communication not only about a teenagers' party which is likely to go on till dawn, but also about proposals for altering or extending a property. Unnecessary ill will, altercations, and even sometimes litigation, can be avoided by neighbours advising and keeping each other informed at the various stages of their projects.

neighbour's planning application

When your neighbour makes an application for planning permission, he does not have to tell you – let alone discuss his plans with you. (In Scotland, an applicant has to notify his immediate neighbours before he makes his application).

In a conservation area, where the local authority have to notify all householders adjoining the site of the proposed development, a notice will be placed somewhere on or near the property, for a period of at least seven days, with details of the proposals.

The notification informs you where, at the local authority, the plans are kept which show the proposed alterations to your neighbour's property. You have a right to inspect these drawings, during normal working hours.

Planning departments often consult neighbours on planning applications which may affect them. Any letter asking for your views will set a date by which you should make them known, preferably in writing.

viewing the plans

Local authority planning departments are required to keep a register of current and previous planning applications available for public inspection.

Anyone has a right to go down to the local authority and examine the drawings, not only when they are submitted with an application for planning permission but for six months after permission has been granted. This is worth remembering: if you think that the works being carried out are not in accordance with the original proposals, you can go back and check.

objecting

Anyone can submit comments to the planning department – you do not need to have a direct interest in the site or be an adjoining owner or occupant. And if the proposal is in a conservation area or the activities suggested are going to affect the environment (possibly by noise or smell), the application may also be advertised in the local newspaper and by a notice on the site. Many authorities send lists of all their planning applications to the local paper and editors publish them.

You are invited to make representations, either in favour or against the proposals of your neighbour. These representations should be made within the time stated in the notification (generally twenty-one days).

If you feel other people will agree with you about a planning application, you can organise a petition and present it to the planning department. Local authorities treat a petition seriously. Make sure the petition is properly set out with its purpose, the reasons for objecting and – legibly – the names and addresses of those signing it. It is better to have a short petition of residents who will actually be affected by the application, than a very long one signed by lots of people including those who live far from the affected area.

The local authority has to consider your comments, and will usually present them, verbatim or in an abbreviated report, to the planning committee. This does not mean that they will allow all objections (knowing that neighbours are reluctant to see properties in their area altered – if only because of the inconvenience this causes).

But you may have good reasons for objecting, such as a question of light restriction, or loss of privacy. Most planning applications for an extension or alteration of a property involve the placing of new windows in a building. If these would seriously affect the privacy that you have enjoyed in your property, you may be able to prevent this by getting the local authority to insist on alterations to the neighbour's plans.

the planning committee

If you have made an objection or a comment to the local planning authority, they may, but do not have to, notify you about the outcome of the application.

The planning committee is made up of a selection of the councillors serving on the local authority. The officers of the local authority recommend to the planning committee the acceptance or rejection of a particular application. The planning committee is not bound always to follow their recommendations, but generally do. If you wish to make a strong case for the rejection of an application, you should lobby your local councillors who are on the planning committee.

Most local authorities' planning committee meetings are open to the public and the press who are allowed to sit in and hear the arguments for and against the proposal and the decision before it is publicised. You are not normally allowed to speak at such meetings but if you have made your views known in advance, you will be able to check that they are taken into account, and also hear any case put forward on the other side.

Some local authorities allow objectors to be heard but you have no right to this. It depends on what the chairman of the committee decides.

Once planning permission has been granted there is no right of objection, or appeal, by anyone other than the applicant. Neighbours, or anyone else, cannot appeal even if directly affected by the outcome of the application.

right to light

Owners of freehold property, and most leasehold property, have a right to light through a window. But do not think that because you will be able to see a new development from your window, this would amount to an actionable injury to your right to light. For that, there would need to be a very real diminution of your light, making your premises noticeably less fit for their use. It would be necessary for the quality of light to a room to have been substantially reduced for there to be a reasonable chance of obtaining compensation for the loss of light. The test is not 'how much light has been taken?' but how much remains. The amount of adequate light in the room must have been reduced to the point where less than half the room is left with adequate light.

If before the development you were able to do *The Times* crossword sitting at a table in the middle of the room, by natural daylight, but afterwards you would not be able to do so (at the same time of day and the same time of year) without switching on the artificial light, your loss of light level may be actionable. You would then be entitled to compensation for the loss of value that your property has suffered as a result.

If a proposed development would cause a loss of light to your property for which you would be entitled to compensation, you may be able to prevent, or hold up building works, by applying to the court for an injunction. But if your claim is not substantiated, you would have to pay compensation to the neighbour, and possibly his building contractors.

ancient lights

'Ancient lights' are a right of light acquired either by uninterrupted enjoyment of light for over twenty years, or by written authority. Once such a right has been established, it cannot be upset and no building should be allowed to interfere with this privilege.

The twenty-year period of enjoyment relates to the property, not to the occupier. So, someone who has recently bought, or moved into, an old building and can prove that a particular window has experienced light in an uninterrupted way for a period of over 20 years, may claim a privilege of 'ancient lights'.

Where there is a vacant piece of land awaiting future development, and the owner wants to prevent neighbours from acquiring rights of light, there is no need to build up a big wall to block out their light. Instead, a 'light obstruction' notice can be registered at the local land charges registry (which is at the local authority's offices). The fee for registering such a notice is at present £32.

right to a view?

Nobody has a right to a view. Provided any building work being planned or carried out does not interfere to a large extent with the right of light, there is nothing that can be done to prevent such work interfering with the view from a particular window.

The fact that your rear windows may look out over rolling countryside, or the bend in the river, is a privilege and not a right. If you do not own the land, however sad you would feel at the loss of a beautiful view, there is little that can be done even if you make an objection relating to the application for planning consent.

nuisance caused by neighbour's building work

You have to expect and accept a certain amount of disruption when your neighbour has the builders in. They should try to keep this to the minimum, and you should try to be tolerant and reasonable.

scaffolding
When scaffolding is erected on any adjoining premises which are in contact with yours, you should be aware of the greater security risk and take whatever precautions you can against burglars.

noise

Construction activities are inherently noisy and often take place in areas which are quiet beforehand and which will be expected to be quiet again after the work has ceased. The Control of Pollution Act 1974 gives local authorities the power to serve a notice with requirements about how the construction works should be carried out so as to minimise noise nuisance. A person intending to have building work done may apply in advance for consent regarding the methods by which the works are to be carried out. Even if he complies with the terms of a notice or a consent, this does not rule out proceedings by a local authority, or an individual, on the grounds of noise nuisance, and also does not constitute a defence to noise abatement proceedings.

builder's radios
The noise caused during normal building operations is unavoidable and is therefore reasonable even though it may disturb you. Music from a radio on the site is avoidable and, therefore, is something that could be classed as unreasonable. First of all, request the builder to reduce the volume; eventually, you could complain to the public health authority to abate the nuisance.

dust

Reasonable precautions should be taken to prevent too much dust being discharged into the air. For example, it is unreasonable to tip large amounts of building rubble through a window onto the ground below.

If you are aggrieved by the amount of dust that appears, complain to the builder or to the neighbour; as a last resort, report the matter to the public health authority as a nuisance.

If the dust has caused damage through the builder's negligence, you could sue for the necessary cost of putting right the damage, such as having to get the front of your property professionally washed down or having to relaunder clothes which were drying on the washing line.

If you have a complaint against the activities of the builder on the adjoining premises, he must be put on notice and be given the opportunity to put right any damage caused. Without such notice, you may lose your own right to claim compensation.

asbestos

Asbestos and asbestos-based products can endanger health in the long term, through breathing in asbestos fibres. The presence of the material in itself is not always a health risk: the risk occurs when asbestos fibres are discharged into the air.

Asbestos has long been used as fire protection and, in older buildings, as an insulation material round pipes and boilers and between the floors of flats. Corrugated asbestos cement sheeting used to be used as roofing material on sheds and concrete garages. When this is to be removed, it should be done without breaking up the sheets, as otherwise small amounts of asbestos dust would be created.

Current public health legislation requires that precautions are taken to prevent discharge of dust containing asbestos into the air.

Asbestos should not be removed by the householder, but by a specialist. A firm employed to remove asbestos has be licensed, under regulations introduced by the Health and Safety Executive in 1984. For advice on dealing with asbestos, contact the environmental health officer of the local authority.

lead

Many older buildings have lead in the paintwork, on the window frames, doors and internal finishes. Removing old lead paint can release the lead as dust into the air. Therefore, the paint should not be removed by *dry* sanding or abrasion.

Dust which may contain lead or asbestos should be bagged, not thrown haphazardly onto a rubbish skip.

The report on *LEAD* in *Which?* August 1984 gives advice on how to reduce lead in your home, and suggests the following safety rules when stripping off old paint

* keep children away
* ventilate the room
* don't rub down with dry sandpaper, especially with a power sander (this creates lead-rich dust)
* don't burn it off with a blow-lamp or blow-torch (this causes fumes)
* do rub down wet (using waterproof abrasive paper) or use a chemical stripper or a hot-air paint stripper which softens the old paint so it can be easily scraped off
* clean up afterwards, vacuum where possible, dispose of paint debris safely by placing it in a strong paper or plastic bag in a dustbin, out of reach of young children. Do not burn it.

fungi

Dry rot, a particularly virulent form of timber infestation, can be spread through airborne spores. It is therefore important that any timber which is affected is destroyed. Ideally, it should be burnt on site, but if this is not practical, the timbers should not just be dropped on to rubbish skips but carefully bagged so that the spores are not discharged into the air.

vibration

The vibrations from building operations in the adjoining property may cause damage to yours. Although some local authorities have equipment for measuring the extent of such vibrations, it would be unusual for the local authority to carry out tests in the case of a private dispute. You would probably have to call in a building surveyor to inspect the condition of your property to see if any fractures or cracks could have been caused by the vibration and therefore be the builder's responsibility. But bear in mind the cost of the surveyor and the uncertainty of the outcome if you sue in such a case.

If drilling or other foundation work is being carried out, which involves vibration of the ground, you should be given advance notice. In exceptional circumstances, it may be necessary for you to move out of your building and the adjoining owner or builder would have to compensate you for losses directly attributable to the work.

right to be told

Many disputes follow from the affront that people feel when a neighbour carries out alterations to his building without telling them. There are some situations where he should notify you, on a personal basis, as distinct from anything the local planning authority may do.

Your neighbour should notify you if the building work that will be carried out

* will affect or touch a wall of your building or the boundary to your property
* will involve digging foundations where the depth of the trench is greater than the distance of the trench from your boundary
* will result in a part of the new building overhanging the line of your boundary.

Certain things do not need planning permission because they are permitted development, and the neighbour need not notify the planning authority – let alone you. These include

* a loft conversion
* a new garden shed or greenhouse
* replacement or erection of a boundary fence not more than one metre in height along a road, or two metres high elsewhere

* small extensions to the property that do not alter the front appearance of the building
* a new small porch at the front of the building.

landlord, repairs and eviction

Lettings by a private landlord which come within the Rent Act 1977 are called regulated tenancies. A regulated tenancy may be protected or statutory. It is protected while it is contractual, that is during the original term of the lease or tenancy agreement, and becomes statutory if the tenant stays on under the Rent Act's security or tenue provisions.

A regulated tenant enjoys a number of rights by virtue of various landlord and tenant laws. Normally, you are not a regulated tenant if the landlord lives in the same house and provides certain services, such as sheets and bedding or cleaning the rooms; also, a 'holiday' letting agreement does not give you a regulated tenancy.

Under the Housing Act 1961, where there is a tenancy of 7 years or less, the landlord is responsible for certain repairs.

responsibility for repairs

Provided you became a tenant after 23 October 1961 and the lease was for 7 years or less, the landlord has to take care of

- repairs to the structure of the building (roof, walls, floors)
- upkeep of gutters, pipes, drains and plumbing (bath, wc. sink basins)
- keeping in good repair the common parts of a shared home, such as the hall-way or common stairways.

Responsibility for other repairs, and for decorations, is divided between the landlord and the tenant, and generally depends on the terms of the lease. The lease is not only the document of title to the property, but also the contract between the landlord and the lessee (that is, the tenant).

If the property is a flat, you will probably share the responsibility for the repair and maintenance of the building with the other leaseholders. The extent of a particular owner's liability for contributions towards the total cost of repair and maintenance is usually set out in the lease.

your responsibility

You have to maintain your property in reasonable order, and the landlord can usually enter your property to see its state of repair – but only after giving you notice that he intends to do so. His right of access to inspect your property is usually set out in the terms and conditions of the lease, which will also set out his right to enforce your liability to repair.

If the landlord wishes you to carry out some repairs to his property which are your liability and you have not done so, he may serve on you a notice of disrepair. This is a list of the defects he has found which you must put right. Normally, he should give you a reasonable period of time within which to carry out the work – say, four months. You have to carry out the repairs if they are your responsibility, but if you are not sure whether they are your responsibility under the terms of your lease, ask a professional advisor to interpret and explain the lease.

what you should do if your home needs repairs

The landlord is only liable to carry out repairs if the tenant gives him notice of the need for repair (unless the landlord actually knows of the defect that needs repairing). Where a defect is the responsibility of the landlord, it is important that you notify him. Do so in writing,

and keep a copy of the letter you sent. You should
● check that the repairs needed are the responsibility of your landlord
● ask your landlord, or the person who collects the rent, to carry out the repairs (you may need proof that you have told your landlord what needs to be done, so even if you made your first request by telephone or in person, follow it up with a letter, and keep a copy; also, keep any letters your landlord sends you)
● give your landlord reasonable time to do the repairs
● if at any stage repairs are done, make a note of the date, which repairs were done, and anything left undone.

if nothing has been done

There are various different steps for getting repairs done that are your landlord's responsibility:

● you can ask your local authority to order your landlord to do the repairs and to take him to court to force him to do so
● you may be able to take the landlord to court yourself
● you can, sometimes, get the work done yourself and deduct the money from the rent.

help from the local authority
Ask the local authority's environmental health inspector to come to your home to see what work is needed. Give your name and address, brief details of your complaint and the name of your landlord. Explain that you have already written to your landlord about the repairs, and that nothing has been done. Make a list of the repairs you want to complain about, and give it to the inspector so that he can then serve a notice on your landlord (that is, an order telling him which repairs he must do).

If your landlord disobeys this order, the local authority can either do the work themselves and claim the cost back from your landlord, or take action against him in court.

statutory nuisance

Under the Public Health Acts, if there is a statutory nuisance, the environmental health inspector may serve an abatement notice, telling the person responsible that he must do repairs and giving him a definite time by which he must finish the work.

There may be a statutory nuisance if your home has any fault or disrepair likely to damage your health or safety such as: damp, leaking roof, unsteady bannisters, rotten floorboards. It may also amount to a nuisance if the house is a danger to the general public or people in adjoining property, for example by damp spreading to the next-door house, or loose slates which might fall from the roof on to the street below, or a rotten window which might fall out into the street.

If the landlord has not done the repairs within the specified time, the local authority will apply to the magistrates' court for a summons.

taking court action yourself

If your landlord fails in his responsibility to keep the structure of your home adequately repaired you can apply to the county court, under section 32 of the Housing Act 1961. You can ask for compensation for damage and inconvenience arising from your landlord not having done repairs, and for an order that the repairs should be done.

The court may, but does not have to, order your landlord to do the work if it thinks this ought to be done, and must award damages if the case is proved – although the damages may be small.

To make a claim for damages you will need:

* copies of the letters you have written to your landlord and any replies from him as evidence that he knew repairs were needed
* photographs of your home showing the state it is in, if possible
* an inspection report giving details of the necessary repairs, if possible
* evidence of any losses or injuries you have suffered because the work was not done.

Before taking the landlord to court, get advice from a solicitor, a citizens advice bureau, a local law centre or housing aid centre. A

32-page booklet, *Your rights to repairs (a guide for private and housing association tenants)* is published by SHAC (the London Housing Aid Centre), 189a Old Brompton Road, London SW5 0AR, price 70p.

There are a number of advantages and disadvantages to taking action yourself. The main advantages are that it can be quicker, and you can claim money for damage to property. The threat of legal action may be enough to prompt your landlord to do the work. The main disadvantages can be the cost to you, and the difficulty of getting adequate proof.

getting the work done yourself

If the repairs that are needed are minor ones, it is sometimes possible to get them done yourself and to deduct the money from the rent. The law is a little uncertain on this, so always get advice first.

You should not simply stop paying rent: if you do this, your landlord will have the legal right to start a court action to evict you for rent arrears. But the landlord cannot simply throw you out.

protection from eviction and harassment

Tenants of furnished or unfurnished houses or flats are protected from being evicted by their landlord. This means that the landlord must prove to a court that he has a legal right to get the accommodation back, before the tenant can be evicted; and the landlord cannot go to court, unless he has followed the procedures laid down by law.

The procedures, and the circumstances under which the landlord will have a legal right to get your accommodation back, vary depending on whether you are a tenant with full protection, with restricted protection, or with basic protection.

You are likely to be a tenant with restricted protection if your landlord has lived in the same house as you have, since your tenancy started.

If you do not fit into the full or restricted protection groups, you will, at the very least, have basic protection. This means that you have a legal right to stay in your accommodation and do not have to leave just because you are asked to by the landlord. He must first get a court hearing and be granted a possession order against you.

basic protection

The basic protection afforded to a residential occupier by the Protection from Eviction Act 1977 arises from two main offences under the Act:

● illegal eviction: it is a criminal offence to unlawfully evict a residential occupier. If your landlord tries to evict you illegally, get advice immediately. Illegal eviction is a criminal offence and the courts have the power to order the landlord to allow you back into your accommodation.

● harassment: it is also a criminal offence for the landlord to do acts calculated to interfere with your peace or comfort, or that of members of your household, or to withdraw services with the intent of trying to get you to move out.

In general, it is difficult to prove that harassment has taken place and that the landlord has acted with intent. The tendency is for the courts to demand a very high standard of proof.

But if you think your landlord has harassed or threatened you, contact an advice centre or ask at your town hall for the tenancy relations (or harassment) officer. Harassment is a criminal offence and the council may be able to take legal action against your landlord.

get advice

Among the booklets published by SHAC is one called *Private tenants: protection from eviction* (price 70p). At the back of it, SHAC says:

> "If anyone is uncertain about particular points affecting their own housing situation or needs, they should contact their local advice centre or SHAC for more detailed information and help.".

maintenance, defects and remedies

Lack of maintenance, or a failure to repair the obvious faults in a house, can lead to major expenses. Sometimes damage is slow to appear. For example, you can end up with dry rot because cracked rainwater pipes have allowed water to penetrate through the walls and dampen the timbers on the inside of the building; or defective guttering or roof coverings can allow water to penetrate which can result in damage to ceilings and internal decorations.

inspect your property

Every property should be examined thoroughly once a year. It is unlikely that you will want to inspect the whole house, from roof to cellar, in one go. But make sure that you will have looked at everything, regularly, outside and inside. Make out your own checklist to make sure that you miss nothing.

Most of this inspection can be carried out with minimal technical knowledge, but a pair of binoculars, a stepladder, and a torch would be useful.

There may be situations where a specialist is needed to determine the full extent of a problem. Your inspection may help you to decide what maintenance work has priority, or it may show up serious faults which should be dealt with promptly, either by an expert, or possibly by you yourself.

REPAIRS CHECKLIST

CHIMNEY pots. Are they cracked or loose, is flaunching sound, is brickwork straight is pointing in good order?
stack

ROOF covering Are there any broken or missing slates or tiles are the flashings sound, Are the ridge or hip tiles secure. Does roof leak?

GUTTERS condition of material, support brackets, is there a fall, do the collect water, are they clean?

DOWNPIPES condition of material, support brackets, clear of debris discharge shoe, grating covers?

VENT PIPES wire balloon to top, brackets?

WALLS WINDOWS decorations, loose putty condition of glass, quality of wood, sill groove clean sub-sill free from cracks?
BRICKWORK pointing quality, condition of bricks, is dampcourse sound, has it been bridged, is brickwork solid or is there a cavity?
CLADDING, is it all in good order?

FENCES boundary fences. whose belong to whom. condit of the material. Special condits. for animals?

HEDGES and TREES pruning. Listing with local authority. ownership & responsibility for maintenance?

PATHS, GATES. condition, risk.?

INTERIOR ROOF SPACE. Is the cold water tank clean, is it insulated, does it have a cover, is the overflow fixed, supported, does it have an adequate fall?
LOFT is it insulated, ventilated, are there any signs of conden-sation?

the chimney

Start at the top, with the chimney stacks. If you have a pair of binoculars, use them to look carefully at the pots to see if they are cracked or fractured. At the base of the pots there should be cementwork immediately above the brickwork of the stack. This should look clean and smooth. If there are extensive cracks in the cement, the pots themselves are probably loose, and a strong wind might blow them over. Those pots are in fact quite heavy; if they fall, they could cause damage to your property as well as being a danger to anyone beneath at the time of the accident.

Put your ear to the chimney breast when there is a strong wind. If you hear a noise like a heavy object being rocked, possibly the pots are rocking on top of the stack – and are in need of repair.

chimney stack

The brickwork beneath the pot should be straight, but it is not unusual to find a slight bend, usually towards the south west due to the effect of wind and sunshine, or a straight lean, due to settlement. If there is more than a slight bend or lean there is a risk of the stack, as well as the pots, falling over. If you are in any doubt about the extent of the lean, the stack should be examined by a builder.

In an older house, the pointing between bricks of the chimney stack can start to decay and either repointing or relaying the bricks is then necessary.

The junction between the chimney stack and the roof covering is usually protected with metal flashing, to prevent water which runs down the face of the roof and the face of the chimney getting into the building through any gaps.

Metal flashing

Flashings are usually made from lead or zinc. Check that there are no splits or cracks in the metal.

Instead of flashing, on an older property, there may be 'listing' (brick, stone, slate or tile projected from the side of the stack) – see if any are split or broken or in need of rebedding.

the roof

Note if there are any slipped or missing tiles or slates, particularly ridge or hip tiles.

Many modern roofs have a felt lining under the tiles which forms a second line of defence against the weather, so that a number of missing tiles may not let the water penetrate. But in a strong wind, more tiles could get lifted off the roof.

When looking at your roof from ground level, note whether the shape of the roof is uneven or out of square. If there are depressions or settlements in the roof surface, it may be wise to get a builder to examine the roof from the inside and to tell you what work is necessary.

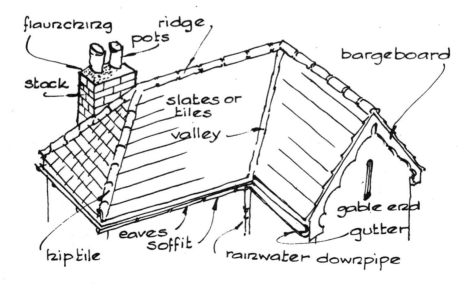

The Which? report published in March 1984 on *How to look after your roof and get it repaired* includes the following warnings of danger signs:

- keep a look out for the occasional slipped slate or tile; if you find one on the ground, investigate where it came from and get it replaced
- large numbers of slipping slates usually indicate that the nails holding them in place are rusted through
- old slates and clay tiles that split into layers will eventually need replacing
- defective pointing in the chimney stack, if not put right, can let in damp or make the chimney unstable
- leaking eaves gutters should be replaced speedily
- valleys and flashings: look out for signs of cracking, or of flashings coming away from the brickwork
- make sure that mortar holding ridge tiles in place is sound.

flat roof

If you need to go onto the surface of the roof to inspect it, be careful where you put your feet. If you tread on the upper sections of the ridges or bubbles on the surface, they may crack and the surface be damaged.

Examine the surface of the covering for any tears or cracks. A flat roof is supported on a timber framework, so it is vital that any leak is dealt with before the timbers are affected by the damp.

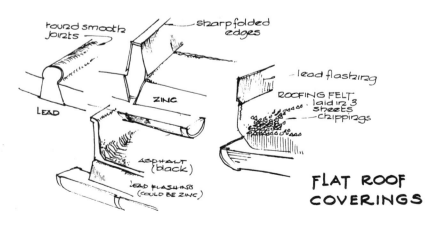

FLAT ROOF
COVERINGS

The flat roof covering may be metal; the condition of the metal can usually be seen around the joints (if zinc) or rolls (if lead). If the zinc is extensively pitted, there is probably some leak. For a lead roof, if you bend bits of lead and find that it cracks along the line of the joint, it has become aged and brittle. (If you experiment with little bits of metal from the roof, around the gutter discharge points, make sure you do not endanger the waterproof covering of your property.)

When the metal has become faulty, the roof surface will require recovering. If it has been leaking, there is likely to be some damage to the timber surfaces underneath.

Leaks on flat roofs can be particularly difficult to trace because the water may travel a long way through the roof before finding an opening. If the roof covering does not have any obvious tears, applying two coats of thick bitumen may stop the leak. Otherwise, a re-felting job may be needed; it is best to leave this to an expert.

guttering

If anything is wrong with the gutters and rainwater down-pipes, water will be discharged over the face of the building, and may eventually penetrate the walls.

The guttering should be cleared out, probably once a year, to remove the debris that collects there. Do this late in the autumn when the leaves have stopped falling and before the winter rains start. Use a trowel to scoop out the accumulation, but while you are working, stuff some rags into the tops of the down-pipes so that the debris will not get pushed down (and do not forget to take them out again when you have finished clearing the guttering). Use a hose or a bucket of water to flush the down-pipes and check they are clear. Fitting a plastic or wire mesh cap over the top of the down-pipe will help to keep it clear.

Watch gutter joints when it is raining, to see whether water is getting out. If so, make a careful note of the exact place so that you can send the builder up to that particular point to carry out a repair.

In dry weather, look out for any rust staining or marks around the joints of metal guttering, or any marks on the face of the brickwork which may show where water has run down.

Check on the quality of the brackets supporting the guttering. When they are old, they may become weakened and allow the guttering to fall or drop out of line.

d-i-y?

If you are working on a roof, remember that it is a long way up. Apart from your own safety, there may be danger to people below who could be injured by falling slates or tools.

Plastic guttering is unable to cope with the weight of a ladder being placed against it, so you would need a ladder stand-off or ladder stay. To get on the roof for working on it, you need a roof ladder which is designed to be wheeled up the roof and hooked onto the ridge. A platform tower is safer than a ladder if heavy objects, such as a large number of tiles, are needed up on the roof.

Such ladders and other equipment can be hired by the day from hire firms.

down-pipes

Down-pipes carry the greater part of the water from the roof's surface. If metal ones are sound, when you tap them with a metal object they will ring true, with a clear ring. If they are faulty, they will give off a very muffled sound.

Look at the condition of the brickwork around the full height of the pipe. Build-up of moss or similar vegetation or green stains on brickwork may be an indication of water having seeped from the pipework.

Some pipes stop six or eight inches above the gully so that water will splash up the face of the wall; eventually these splashes can result in water penetrating through the wall, causing damage to the interior of the property. To prevent damage, paint the portion of wall that gets splashed with a masonry water-proofing liquid containing silicone.

windows

The wind imposes substantial pressure on a building, and water may be driven up a window frame and through any gaps. In some cases, where the putty securing the glass to the frame is faulty, water can be driven around the glass.

Examine all frames for this: if the putty is damaged, cracked or dried out, water will run behind it and into the framework of the window, eventually rotting a wooden frame.

Check on the condition of wooden window frames. Push the surface of the paint with a blunt screwdriver or pen knife, to see whether the wood has become very soft.

Window frames of aluminium or uPVC (unplasticised polyvinyl chloride) need little or no maintenance and should need no attention within the first twenty years. Even after that, any maintenance would be in order to improve the appearance rather than to deal with decay.

Where there are double-glazed windows, especially those on south-facing walls, check for moisture or mould growth in between the glass, which may indicate a breakdown of the sealant, or a hairline crack in the inner or outer pane. Remember that the replacement of the windows may be covered by your buildings insurance policy: claim, unless it is specifically excluded.

the windowsill

When it rains and the water runs down the pane, it should splash onto the windowsill and be thrown clear of the wall underneath the window, to drip beyond the face of the brickwork or other external finish. If it splashes onto the wall, it will stain the wall and the damp may eventually penetrate.

Gently apply a blunt screwdriver to the window sill and if the surface seems faulty, check the inside of the wall at this point. If it has been wallpapered, the paper will become soft and loose if water has penetrated.

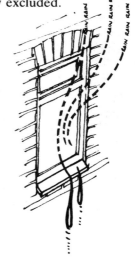

Wooden sills should have a drip groove on the underside to ensure that water cannot track back on the brickwork below the window. Check to see that it is clear and if it is not, rake it out.

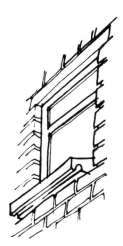

brickwork

Some types of brick in older houses have poor weathering properties and when the surfaces erode or disintegrate, the softer inner part of the brick becomes exposed; water can then penetrate and cause damage to the inside of the property. You should get these bricks cut out and replaced or refaced (which is expensive).

Brickwork soaks up water when it rains and discharges this water by evaporation, when the sun eventually shines. Some of the water will run down the face of the wall, and if the brick jointing or pointing is in poor condition, the water may soak into the wall.

Pointing is the strip of mortar which fixes brick to brick. It should be flush with the surface of the bricks. If it becomes rough and irregular, water will collect on the brick face. Rub the surface of the joints with your finger and see if they are soft: the mortar should feel firm but not too hard and should not crumble away. If the wall has been repointed in the past with a hard mixture of cement, this will break off in long lines, and water will run behind the space of the pointing and enter the brickwork.

Well-built brickwork generally needs little maintenance apart from repointing. This could be a d-i-y job but it is time-consuming and fiddly: getting a slice of mortar neatly and cleanly into the joint needs precision and a steady hand.

If there is an area of rendering on your house, inspect it for cracks. Water may get behind the render and loosen it from the wall. This should be remedied immediately, otherwise more water will get in. Rendering is a job best left to the specialist.

cavity walls

A cavity wall is formed by two 'skins' (walls of brick or blockwork), with a narrow space between the inner and outer skin. Because the outer brickwork is separated from the inner wall, water does not penetrate through the full thickness of the wall, as happens in older properties which have solid outside walls.

The cavity, which is an air gap, also provides some insulation. In many modern houses, the insulation has been enhanced by filling the space with insulating material. The two walls are held together by metal brackets – called wall ties. In a few houses, built before 1979, the wall ties have been found to rust and expand, causing the brick joints to open slightly where the ties are fixed. It is unlikely that your house will be affected, but you should check. If you find horizontal cracks around your building, at about 18 inch (450 mm) intervals, it is possible that this is the cause. It would need expert attention.

damp-proof course

To prevent moisture from rising up the walls from the ground below, all houses built since 1875 have a damp-proof course (dpc). This is a horizontal waterproof membrane which separates the brickwork below the surface of the ground, from the dryer part of the house above the ground. Without it, water would be able to rise up through the brickwork, and the walls in lower rooms would be damp.

It is important that this damp-proof course is never bridged. (From outside, it looks like a thicker section of horizontal pointing between the bricks.) Make sure that the soil in any flower bed near the house is not piled up against the walls of the building above the course. Similarly, if the surface of a patio, or outside steps or pathway is above the level of the damp-proof course, it would be bridged and water could continue to rise up the wall.

If water seeps into the floor, from faulty plumbing perhaps, it will lie on top of the damp-proof membrane and then spread across the ground floor. It may become visible some distance away from the original leak, which may have been from the connection to the back of a washing machine, or dishwasher or similar appliance that has been leaking for some time. When you inspect your appliances, have a good look behind them to make sure that there are no leaks.

airbricks

A timbered ground floor has to have ventilation to ensure that conditions beneath it do not get damp enough for rot to start. Ventilation bricks, or air-bricks as they are called, allow the air to move through the underside of the floor. These bricks, close to ground level, must be kept unobstructed and clear, so remove any debris which may have collected in the holes. If the ventilation is through grilles, similarly make sure that they are kept clean. If there is no ventilation, the timbers of the ground floor will become damp and there is a strong likelihood of dry rot or other fungal decay.

Damaged or broken air-bricks will not affect the movement of air through the floor, but might allow mice to get into the property.

the loft

If you have a pitched roof, tap the surface of black felt under the roof covering, to find out if there is any loose material lying on the external side, between the felt and slates or tiles. If you can hear pieces of loose material running down on the outside of the felt, it may indicate that some of the tiles on the roof are damaged. If there is no felt, you can check the tiles or slates by just looking. Daylight is the main thing to look for: do not do the inspection after dark.

Be careful where you put your feet if there is no flooring; step only on joists, and preferably not at their centre.

It is a mistake to seal the surface of the roof and all the openings around the eaves. Everyday living in a house creates moisture and a great deal of warmth: the warm damp air drifts upwards and will end up in the roof space. If there is no ventilation, the water content of the air will condense, and settle on the surface or underside of the roof's covering, and the damp may spread to the woodwork.

Insulation within the roof space is important to preserve as much warmth of the house as possible, but do not put insulation directly under the cold water storage cistern, otherwise the water might freeze over in cold weather.

If the cistern is of galvanised metal, check if there is corrosion around the seams and joints. You may need a mirror and a torch to examine the underside of a cistern. If there is rust or corrosion, call in a plumber to advise you whether you should replace the cistern.

Check the ball or float valve, which controls the water in the cistern. The float rises and falls with the water and opens and closes a valve. Older metal balls tend to take on water, so that their ability to float declines and eventually the valve no longer operates and the cistern will begin to overfill. The overflow pipe should discharge this surplus water to the outside of the building. A dripping overflow pipe should alert the householder to the probable failure of the ball-valve.

condensation

Condensation occurs when warm air, which holds more moisture than cold air, meets a cool surface and releases some of its moisture. Condensation is less likely where there is good ventilation, adequate constant heating and good insulation.

Condensation is most likely to occur in a steamy kitchen and bathroom. However careful you are, a lot of water vapour is inevitable in the kitchens and bathroom and, even if your heating and insulation are adequate, you are unlikely to prevent condensation altogether. A room heated by paraffin or a flueless gas heater (bottled gas) is also a likely place because the fuel creates moisture. Unheated rooms such as bedrooms, particularly if exposed to cold winds, are likely to have condensation.

A mild misting over of windows will probably not cause harm, but in severe cases, streaming walls that never dry out may become spotted with mould, and water may run down walls and windows, behind skirting and on to window frames, causing them to rot.

cutting down condensation
It is possible to reduce the likelihood of condensation by:

- keeping kitchen and bathroom doors shut
- drying clothes outside (or in a vented tumble drier)
- putting lids on saucepans
- not letting the kettle boil a long time

Opening a window helps minor problems; fitting an extractor fan which actually removes the moisture-laden air and draws in dry air from the rest of the house is a better solution.

woodworm

The most likely places where there may be signs of woodworm attack are in the roof space, in skirting and floor boards, in an understairs cupboard and – particularly – in woodwork that may be damp, such as the area behind and under sinks and the bath, around the wc, basement or cellar. Woodworm is also found in plywood and wickerwork, and can attack furniture.

The critical period during which to look for signs of active woodworm infestation is between May and September, when the furniture beetle emerges from the wood. It comes through small perfectly circular holes, about two millimetres in diameter: the hole has a sharp outline and shows clean light wood inside, and there may be fresh-looking dust spilling out of the holes. If you find round holes that look dull and weathered, they may be a sign of an old, no longer active, attack. Larger oval holes, generally filled with dust and spaced widely apart, are a sign of a different species (long horn beetle); if you suspect them, you should seek expert advice.

Altogether, it is worth seeking advice for treating woodworm; there are d-i-y treatments in the form of insecticidal fluid, to be applied to or injected into the wood, but it is an unpleasant and not altogether straightforward task.

wet and dry rot

Both dry rot and wet rot attack wood and cause it to disintegrate. Dry rot is the more serious of the two.

wet rot

Wet rot can exist only if there is a source of moisture, such as contact with damp brickwork; if the wood dries out, the fungus dies.

The problem is localised by the need for moisture. Wet rot is likely to occur anywhere that is persistently wet. It is most commonly found in roof timbers where the roof leaks, in damp cellars and basements that never get a chance to dry out, in areas where faulty plumbing causes the wood to get very wet, and in the corners of window frames where water from rain or heavy condensation collects.

Wet rot will be stopped if the source of damp is eliminated and the wood allowed to dry out thoroughly and quickly. Central heating and improved ventilation will both help. All badly damaged timbers should be removed and replaced with wood that has been pre-treated with preservative.

If an attack of wet rot is discovered in its very early stages, before the wood has been severely weakened, it may be possible to remedy it by applying a fungicidal solution. Watch carefully for further signs of rot.

dry rot

Dry rot is found typically in cellars, basements and understairs cupboards, under floors and behind panelling.

Dry rot 'controls' its surroundings, generating the moisture that it requires; if ventilation is poor, it can spread very rapidly. If there is little or no ventilation, it can penetrate not only timber but plaster and brickwork and it can pass over metal, stone and concrete. It is not enough merely to eliminate the source of the damp: badly affected timber must be removed and destroyed, and adjacent areas – including brickwork and masonry – treated with fungicide.

Because dry rot tends to attack in unventilated spaces, it is often not suspected until floorboards start to give way. Where you suspect dry rot, check for the following signs:

* a damp 'mushroomy' smell
* warped surface wood, which sounds hollow when tapped
* wood which has darkened in colour and split into cubes
* fine reddish powder or cottonwool-like strands
* wood that has become dry and light in weight and can be crumbled to a powder between the fingers.

Some of these symptoms may, of course, mean something completely different. Wood that sounds hollow, for example, can indicate particular methods of construction.

not a d-i-y job

Dry rot requires drastic remedies. As well as eliminating the source of damp and replacing damaged timber, all infected timber has to be removed and plaster stripped to expose the full extent of the fungal infestation. All timber in the area must be treated and all infected brickwork and masonry sterilised.

It is not easy to establish the full extent of dry rot: you should get an expert to help you.

Be wary of the specialist firm of timber contractors who offers to treat woodworm or rot in timbers which are too weak for their purpose. Treatment will not add mechanical strength to timbers. There comes a time when badly decayed timbers need to be replaced. Treatment in such cases is a waste of money. New timbers should always be pre-treated, as a precaution.

Most of the specialist firms dealing with dry rot, wet rot and woodworm, are members of the British Wood Preserving Association, 150 Southampton Row, London WC1B 5AL.

Damp treatment is carried out by members of the British Chemical Damp Course Association, P.O.B. 105, Reading, Berks, RG3 6NG.

Members of these associations all give a guarantee which is backed up by the Guaranteed Treatments Protection Trust Ltd., so that if the firm should go bankrupt, the guarantee is not worthless, and will be honoured.

calling in expert help

Where you find that something is wrong with your property, particularly if you do not know the cause, you may need to call in an expert such as a timber specialist, plumber, electrician, heating engineer, local builder, surveyor, architect.

What you expect is:

* an indication of the cause of the problem
* advice about its possible extent
* advice about the necessary remedial work and repairs which should be carried out
* the cost.

The specialist may also be able to give you advice about methods of funding (such as insurance claims, grants or a claim against a third party).

inspection

Before instructing someone to carry out an inspection, you should be aware of what this may cost. Most of the tradesmen such as a builder or timber specialist carry out the inspection free of charge, and submit an estimate for the remedial work. For them, it is a service they provide in the hope that you will ask them to carry out the necessary work.

If you employ a surveyor he will charge a fee for his inspection: ask him to let you know the extent of his inspection, and the fee that he will charge.

inadequate or wrong advice

It is important that you tell the individual whom you consult exactly what advice you expect. If you ask a builder to look at the drains, he will have no responsibility for failing to comment on the roof.

A professional owes his client a duty of care; the standard of expertise required from him is that expected from the average specialist dealing with the specific problems. You can claim professional negligence if, as a result of the expert failing in his duty of care, you have suffered a loss (financial or physical).

You do not automatically have a claim against a specialist who gives you incorrect advice. It would have to be shown that he was negligent in the way he examined the property, or in the interpretation of the evidence available to him.

surveyor's omission

In the case of a surveyor, professional negligence may be caused by an omission, for example, failing to notice a crack in a wall, or not recording that roof slates were missing.

Reporting a defect in a property is not enough without warning you of the likely consequences, for example to report that there is a leaking rainwater pipe, without also indicating that this may lead to dry rot. A comment that woodworm is present in timbers of the ground floor is not enough information. The householder needs to know whether there is a substantial infestation and what the likely cost of putting it right will be.

Certain types of building design have a known history of problems. Even if there is nothing to suggest, during the course of an ordinary examination, that this problem is present in your property, the expert should advise you of the known poor track-record and the risk of such problems in this type of building.

Similarly, where an old property still has its original roof while the adjoining properties have been re-roofed, the inspector should warn that it is highly likely that the roof of your property may require repairs within a few years.

complaint

Make your complaint as soon as you notice – even if that is long after the inspection or long after the work has been carried out. Generally, the time limit is six years from when the damage becomes evident. If you complain shortly after you receive the report, it may be fairly easy to prove this negligence: a photograph of the roof, or of a wall, may be all that is needed. Where the complaint is made some time after the report, it becomes more difficult: a crack which is evident in the wall two years after the inspection, may not have been there at the time of the original visit. The extensive staining round a rainwater pipe, which is now clear to see, may not have been sufficiently major to be picked up in the original inspection.

finding a specialist

Generally, contacting a trade association or professional organisation can be a useful source of further information or the first step in finding a specialist. Some of these organisations will also pursue complaints about their members.

Aluminium Window Association
26 Store Street,
London WC1E 7EL
telephone: 01-637 3578

Association of Noise Consultants
6 Long Lane
London EC1A 9DP
telephone: 01-606 1461

Brick Development Association
Woodside House
Winkfield
Windsor
Berkshire SL4 2DX
telephone: 0344 885651

British Board of Agrément
PO Box 195, Bucknalls Lane
Garston
Watford WD2 7NG
telephone: 0923 670844

**British Chemical Dampcourse
   Association**
PO Box 105
Reading
Berkshire RG3 6NG
telephone: 0734-24911

British Decorators Federation
6 Haywra Street
Harrogate
North Yorkshire HG1 5BL
telephone: 0423 67292

British Wood Preserving Association
150 Southampton Row
London WC1B 5AL
telephone: 01-837 8217

Building Research Advisory Service
Building Research Establishment
Garston
Watford WD2 7JR
telephone: 0923 676612

no charge for short enquiries (hourly charge if more complex, and site visit)

Princes Risborough Laboratory
Princes Risborough
Aylesbury
Buckinghamshire HP17 9PX
telephone: 08444 3101

You can get names of independent consultants from advisory service

Chartered Institute of Arbitrators
75 Cannon Street
London EC4N 5BH
telephone: 01-236 8761

Draught Proofing Advisory Association Ltd
PO Box 12
Haslemere
Surrey GU27 3AN
telephone: 0428 54011

External Wall Insulation Association
PO Box 12
Haslemere
Surrey GU27 3AN
telephone: 0428 54011

Faculty of Architects and Surveyors
15 St Mary Street
Chippenham
Wiltshire SN15 3JN
telephone: 0249 655398

Felt Roofing Contractors' Advisory Board
Maxwelton House
Boltro Road
Haywards Heath
Sussex RH16 1BJ
telephone: 0444 51835

Fencing Contractors' Association
7-15 Lansdowne Road
Croydon CR9 2PL
telephone: 01-688 4422

Guaranteed Treatments Protection Trust Ltd
PO Box 77
27 London Road
High Wycombe
Buckinghamshire HP11 1BW
telephone: 0494 447049

Glass and Glazing Federation
6 Mount Row
London W1Y 6DY
telephone: 01-409 0545

Heating and Ventilating Contractors Association
Esca House
34 Palace Court
London W2 4JG
telephone: 01-229 5543

**Incorporated Association of
Architects and Surveyors**
Jubilee House
Billing Brook Road
Western Favell
Northampton NN3 4NW
telephone: 0604 404121

Institute of Plumbing
Scottish Mutual House
North Street
Hornchurch
Essex RM11 1RV
telephone: 04024 72791

**Metal Roofing Contractors'
Association**
Hamlyn House
Highgate Hill
London N19
telephone: 01-272 0233

**National Association of Plumbing,
Heating and Mechanical Services
Contractors**
6 Gate Street
London WC2A 3NX
telephone: 01-405 2678

**National Cavity Insulation
Association**
PO Box 12
Haslemere
Surrey GU27 3AN
telephone: 0428 54011

**National Federation of Roofing
Contractors**
15 Soho Square
London W1V 5FB
telephone: 01-439 1753

National Self-Builders Association
Chelston House
Flower Lane
Amesbury
Wiltshire SP4 7HE
telephone: 0980 22933

Royal Institute of British Architects
66 Portland Place
London W1N 4AD
telephone: 01-580 5533

**Royal Institution of Chartered
Surveyors**
12 Great George Street
London SW1P 3AD
telephone: 01-222 7000

Scottish Decorators Association
249 West George Street
Glasgow G2 4RB
telephone: 041-221 7090

**Thermal Insulation Contractors'
Association**
24 Ormond Road
Richmond
Surrey TW10 6TH
telephone: 01-948 4151

**The Timber Research and
Development Association**
Hughenden Valley
High Wycombe
Buckinghamshire HP14 4ND
telephone: 024024 2771
will answer simple problems you
have about wood and wood-based
materials. A charge will be made if
investigation is necessary.

employing a builder

A firm or individual can use the word 'building contractor' without having experience of, or qualifications in, the responsibilities and methods required in constructing or altering property.

Local knowledge and recommendations from friends or acquaintances may be a useful guide to finding a good firm, but this is not infallible. Firms of builders are only as good as the people who work on individual sites, including the people who supervise them.

These organisations may be able to give you a list of their members in your area:

Federation of Master Builders
33 John Street
London WC1N 2BB
telephone: 01-242 7583

an association of about 20,000 small and medium-sized building firms; all member firms have employer's liability and public liability insurance.

The FMB has introduced a national register of warranted builders and through its regional lists of member firms can supply you with names of local builders specialising in one type of building.

To get onto the warranty register, a builder has to provide references from several sources such as banks and insurance companies and needs to have three years' consecutive trading experience immediately before applying to join, and has to be a member of the FMB.

Clients who have work done under the warranty get a two-year guarantee against defects due to faulty workmanship or materials.

Work of clearly a temporary nature and not intended to be warranted for a period of two years is excluded – such as repairs of storm damage, or temporary roof covering. Roof work, other than complete renewal of the slate or tile covering is also excluded.

The two-year guarantee starts from the date on which the account is settled, if that is within 21 days of it being presented. The guarantee is underwritten by an insurance company and will cover building work valued up to £30,000. The insurance premium is paid by the builder.

The Building Employers' Confederation
82 New Cavendish Street
London W1M 8AD
telephone: 01-580 5588

a trade association of building firms from the very large to the very small; it exists to serve the needs of the member firms by providing representation and legal, technical and advice services. Regional offices of the BEC can provide lists of builders who carry out small-scale works, such as extensions.

The National Home Enlargement Bureau
PO Box 67
High Wycombe
Bucks HP15 6XP
telephone: 0494 711649

an organisation which aims to give help on home enlargements; has lists of builders, builders' merchants and insurance brokers in your area. Also runs the register of bonded builder scheme, which is intended to help the consumer find good builders. The customer has the option of making his contract the subject of a contract-completion guarantee, backed by insurance.

obtaining a price from a builder

For the builder to be able to produce an accurate price which he can work to, he needs clear instructions of your requirements.

When writing to a builder for a price, use the correct terms and phrases. Asking for an 'estimate' from a builder does *not* mean the price to carry out a job: an estimate is no more than a guide to what the price may be, and does not mean that he will necessarily carry out the work at that figure.

You should ask either for his 'tender' for the cost of carrying out the work, or for his quotation. Tender implies he is competing with others; quotation does not always mean this. In a quotation, the conditions should be stated, in so far as they are not standard ones.

tender

is the offer made by a builder to carry out specific work for a named sum of money; it does not include itemised details of cost.

specification

describes proposed building operations in terms of workmanship, supplementing the drawings that are attached to it; it should list the materials that are to be used (such as a specific bathroom suite, a particular type of tap or door handle).

bill of quantities

is used solely for obtaining competitive tenders, usually for large complex projects.

schedule of works

lists the items of work to be carried out within a particular contract. This is normally attached to a specification which lists the quality of material to be used. The builder's quotation for carrying out the work is based on these documents.

variations

are changes to or deviations from the work specified in the contract, irrespective of whether the change is in the scope, the type of work or the materials which are to be used. The builder is not entitled to extra money if the variation is caused by defective workmanship on his part: he has to correct this at his own cost.

sub-contractor

individual or firm appointed by the main contractor to carry out parts of the work on his behalf – electrical installation, plastering, decorating, bricklaying; he is, effectively a workman of the builder, who is responsible for paying him and for the quality of the sub-contractor's work.

'nominated' sub-contractor

If you want a particular firm or person to carry out certain elements of a building operation, this fact should be included in the original contract. The builder then includes in his price the price submitted by the nominee, plus an element for his profit; the builder may disclaim liability for the quality of the nominee's workmanship.

provisional sum

sum included in a specification to cover the cost of carrying out certain parts of the work, where there is insufficient information for an accurate price (perhaps the details of particular bathroom or sanitary fittings); when the information is to hand, the builder includes the net cost of the goods, and adds his overhead charges and profit.

prime cost sum ('p.c.' sum)

basic cost before the builder has added his profit and overhead charges; it is usually incorporated in a specification for work of a specialist contractor outside the normal sphere of the builder's experience. For example, if the work includes the installation of a damp-proof course, the 'p.c.' sum would be the quotation from various specialist contractors. The builder will then add to that figure his overhead charges, and profit.

contract

A contract for building operations may be on a pre-printed form such as that supplied by the Royal Institution of Chartered Surveyors or the Royal Institute of British Architects.

A contract does not have to be in writing. If you have called in a builder to put a new window in your kitchen in place of the existing one, and he said that he will do this work for £200, a contract has been formed when you say "Yes, go ahead." An oral contract is just as binding, although more difficult to enforce, as one set out in writing.

A written contract does not have to be formal, but should set out

* the work to be carried out
* the method of carrying it out
* the time within which it is to be completed
* costs
* payment to be made to the builder
* conditions, including what is to happen if the work is not completed as agreed.

The *Which? book of home improvements and extensions* includes a section on 'Contract with a builder', with suggested clauses for a fixed-price contract.

The main considerations are time, cost and standard of work.

time

When the builder submits his quotation, he should tell you the time he will require to carry out the work, and also tell you when he will be ready to start – be it next week, or four months hence. Quotations are often given two or three months before the builder is ready to start work.

extra time and extra cost

His estimate of time taken will be on the basis that the work is that which has been specified. If you ask for a large number of variations and extra work to be done after the builder has started, extra time and extra cost will accrue.

It is a good idea to keep a daily record of any extra work that you ask your builder to do, and the approximate cost, so that at the end of the job you know how much extra was involved on top of the original agreement.

The builder is not responsible for delays caused by factors over which he has no control – for example, if there is a national strike of building employees or if you have selected materials which are not readily available.

Often it is not possible to determine all the work that will be required before work starts, because some parts affected by the work are concealed. Any extra should be carried out at a cost comparable with what was agreed for similar work within the original quotation.

As a rule, it is advisable to get a written quotation for each variation or extra piece of work to be carried out. If this rule were to be strictly followed, however, there would be major disturbance to the flow of work, which itself might incur extra cost because of the delays that would be caused. But you should at all stages ask what anything extra is going to cost, even if the builder can tell you only approximately.

standard of work

The one essential over which there can be no dispute is that the work as carried out should be suitable and satisfactory for the functions it is designed to perform. It has to be reasonable, but does not have to be of the highest quality.

It is important that you agree before the work starts the quality that you require and are paying for.

sub-contracting
A firm of builders will only be able to employ people whom they can retain in full work. Few retain the services of all the tradesmen throughout the year. In many cases, a contractor may only retain two or three people as his own direct employees and get the other tradesmen from some other firm: bricklayers from one, the joiners from another, the electricians and the plumbers may be self-employed or from other independent firms specialising in this type of work.

The standard of work achieved may therefore vary from year to year or job to job; the people used on contract may be different ones from those that the same builder had retained for his last building job.

Before employing a particular builder, ask how many and which of his workmen are going to be sub-contractors. You may wish to reconsider engaging a builder on the strength of good work previously done by one of his workmen if he is now sub-contracting the job to someone else.

Office of Fair Trading

A report by the Director General of Fair Trading, published in June 1983 on *Home Improvements* starts with these 'golden rules for householders':

● **before you start**

– *decide exactly what you want done. For larger jobs, consider getting professional advice from an architect or surveyor.*

● **local regulations**

– *ask your local authority if you need planning permission or building regulations approval. You may be able to get a grant.*

● **shop around**

– *don't be rushed: get estimates or quotations in writing from at least two firms.*

● **the firm**

– *find out as much as you can about the firm and whether it is competent to carry out the work. If in doubt, get a second opinion.*

- **your contract**

- *make sure your contract is in writing and gives full details of prices, cancellation rights, guarantees (and how long they last), and when the work will be finished. Check whether any sub-contractors are being used and who is liable if things go wrong.*

- **payment**

- *be careful about parting with money in advance or paying excessive deposits. Always question any increases in price and ask why they were not included in the original estimate.*

- **if a problem arises**

- *act quickly and get advice quickly from a Citizens Advice Bureau or Trading Standards Department.*

The following are extracts from recommendations in the report:

competition
3.8 There are no restrictions on entry to the home improvements industry – any individual can establish himself as a builder, decorator, plumber or electrician without training or experience. The industry is fragmented: there are many trade associations in the sector, many representing no more than a small percentage of any particular trade. Trade associations could do much more to set standards of competency and skill and to publicise their members' adherence to professional standards. In practice, the householder has to rely on claims made by traders and on previous experience or recommendation when deciding on the capability and reliability of any particular firm or individual.

statements made by salesmen
4.16 The various claims and representations made before agreement is reached on a transaction are likely to be important factors in the householder's decision. Some information may be given in sales literature but frequently oral statements are made which go beyond the scope of the literature. If information about a particular product is false or incomplete it is impossible for householders to make either a proper decision or fair and

accurate comparisons. Against this background it is particularly objectionable for traders to seek to disown by way of contractual terms, such as 'the terms in the contract may only be waived or varied in writing by a Director of the Company', any statements made by the salesman outside his authority. These terms may be of limited legal effect but can seriously mislead consumers.

4.18 The terms 'estimate' and 'quotation' as used in the home improvements field are often confused and used interchangeably by both traders and householders. An estimate should be an oral or written approximation of how much a job will cost, which may or may not be an accurate reflection of the final bill, whereas a quotation should be an itemised breakdown of charges which will not be exceeded. Increases in costs between an estimate and the final bill can be unjustifiable, such as the addition of items which should reasonably have been included in the original price, or justifiable, such as those arising from unforeseeable structural defects which need to be remedied before the commissioned work can be completed satisfactorily. Householders need to know whether traders are tendering to do the work at a fixed price, come what may, or simply giving an idea of the likely cost. They should ask traders to provide an itemised written list which specifies the work to be carried out, when it will be done and that the prices stated will not be exceeded without the householder's specific authorisation, as this will afford them some protection, no matter whether the trader calls his document an estimate or a quotation.

delays
6.1 Delays, both in starting to carry out work and in completing it, are a perennial problem. A householder, once committed to a transaction, is anxious for the work to be completed as soon as possible, and delay in starting and completing work coupled with the dirt, noise and general untidiness that seem inevitably to accompany many home improvement and repair jobs do much to give the industry an unsatisfactory image. The irritation and inconvenience caused are compounded by traders who are reluctant to explain why delays occur even when there are perfectly reasonable explanations, such as bad weather.

sub-contractors

6.4 Many home improvements contracts require the use of several different skills. Rewiring a house may require a plasterer to make good the walls, while a new plumbing system may require an electrician to assist in the connection of an immersion heater; consequently many traders either use or recommend the use of other tradesmen to complete work. Householders, however, sometimes experience difficulty in such situations because it is not always clear where responsibility lies if things go wrong and from whom to seek redress.

6.6 When work is sub-contracted, the contractor is legally responsible for the work done by the sub-contractor, and the householder has adequate rights to sue the contractor if the work is done badly by a sub-contractor. Where the main contractor recommends another contractor to do part of the work, so that the householder makes a separate contract with the sub-contractor, the householder's only recourse in the event of unsatisfactory work is against the sub-contractor. There may be exceptions to this if the householder can prove that the contractor made a negligent recommendation as to the sub-contractor's capabilities, or if the terms of the relevant contract are such that the householder can sue both contractor and sub-contractor for defective work. The Office recommends that, where the main contractor is intending that sub-contractors should carry out specific parts of the work, this should be made known to the householder.

sub-standard workmanship

6.7 Many comments were made about the problem of sub-standard workmanship. Such complaints are not confined to any one area of home improvements or to any particular size of firm. Contractors are not always to blame for these complaints. A householder may have unjustifiably high expectations of the end results of a job, or may not appreciate that unforeseen problems can arise. In home improvements, as in other contracts for goods and services, cheap remedies can prove unsatisfactory in the long term. Some problems arise simply because of misunderstandings between householders and traders, but there is undoubtedly a minority of traders throughout the industry which persistently fails to meet the standards legitimately expected by householders and the rest of the industry.

redress

9.1 It is inevitable that in home improvements and building work some jobs will prove to be unsatisfactory, giving rise to disputes, and adequate procedures for resolving such disputes are therefore essential. Too often consumers are reluctant to press their complaints, even when justified, because the problems they can encounter appear so daunting. And many consumers perceive that taking their case to court can be costly in terms of both time and money. Nevertheless, as the discussion paper said, greater confidence on the part of householders in securing effective redress would contribute to raising standards among traders.

codes of practice

11.4 Voluntary codes of practice cannot directly control the activities of traders who do not belong to trade associations. They do, however, help to set standards within an industry and act as a reference point for acceptable trading practices. As more companies abide by codes of practice, householders will tend to expect the same standards from non-members. It is essential, therefore, that all the trade associations in the home improvements industry ensure that householders are well informed about the standards they should expect, and that they understand the benefits of trading with companies which belong to trade associations which have adopted codes of practice. Member companies should make known their membership by using the trade association's logo on their business premises and on all their documents.

claiming on insurance

In order to insure anything, you have to have an insurable interest – namely, that you are responsible for the goods and would suffer financially from their destruction. In order to have a claim on an insurance policy, you must be able to show that you have suffered a loss *and* that the loss was caused by an insured peril, and did not fall into one of the exclusions. For household insurance, 'perils' are the events (listed in the policy) which can cause loss or damage to a property.

Nearly all insurance policies exclude liability for damage caused by radioactivity or as a result of war; in addition to this, most sections of buildings insurance policies have their own exclusions. And many sections of insurance policies specify an excess, that is an amount which is not paid by the insurers but has to be borne by the insured person himself.

Policies vary also with regard to cover for outbuildings such as a garage, and whether walls and fences are covered. But in general, all buildings policies insure you for damage or loss caused by the following:

* fire
  likely exclusion: smoke damage where there have been no flames or burning
* explosion, lightning, earthquake, thunderbolt
* storm, tempest, flood
  likely exclusions: damage to gates, walls, fences, hedges
  likely excess: the 'first' £15 of every claim

* theft, and attempted theft
  includes damage done by burglar
  likely exclusion: no cover when the property is left unoccupied
  (that is, not being lived in)
* riot, civil commotion, strike, labour disturbances
* damage by malicious persons or vandals
  likely exclusion: no cover when the property is left unoccupied
* leakage of oil from storage tank, pipe, fixed heating installation
  likely exclusion: no cover when the property is left unoccupied
  likely excess: the 'first' £10 or £15 of every claim
* water overflowing or escaping from tanks, apparatus, or pipes
  likely exclusion: no cover when the property is left unoccupied
  likely excess: the 'first' £10 or £15 of every claim
  damage caused *by* water (or oil) is covered, but damage *to* the
  pipes or other vessel is not always covered
* frost, freezing of water
  likely exclusions: damage to pools, dry stone walls, patios, drives
  and paths, gates, fences and hedges, and while the property is left
  unoccupied
  likely excess: the 'first' £15 of every claim
* subsidence or heave of the site on which the building stands, and
  land slip
  likely exclusions: damage caused by the demolition of a building,
  by erosion, by structural alteration or repair, by bedding down of
  a new structure, by faulty workmanship or the use of defective
  materials; also, in most policies, damage to boundary walls,
  patios, drives and paths, fences and hedges unless the main
  building is also damaged at the same time
  likely excess: up to £500 or 3% or 5% of the cost of completely
  rebuilding the house
* damage caused by the breakage or collapse of television aerial or
  other aerials
  likely exclusions: damage done to the aerial or mast itself (but this
  may be covered by the contents policy)

★ impact (by any vehicle, or animal; in some policies, also by falling trees, telegraph poles, lamp posts)
likely exclusions: fences and gates
likely excess: the first £25 of any claim if damage is caused by your own car, or a member of your family's
★ accidental breakage of fixed glass and sanitary fittings
likely exclusions: no cover when the property is left unoccupied; breakage of something that was already cracked
★ accidental damage to cables or underground service pipes supplying the property
but only those for which you are legally responsible
★ professional fees
(that is, architect, surveyor, consultant or lawyer necessarily employed when the building has to be rebuilt or repaired); also the cost of removing the debris and the additional costs of rebuilding to comply with statutory or local by-law requirements.
★ loss of rent
what it would cost to stay elsewhere if your house is uninhabitable as a result of one of the insured perils for which you also make an insurance claim
likely limit: 10% of sum insured.

contents insurance

The contents of your home can be insured as part of the same policy as the building, or through a separate contents insurance policy. The perils are very similar to what is covered by a buildings policy, but apply to household goods, furnishings, appliances and personal effects. If your home is rented, a contents policy includes some cover for a tenant's responsibility for his landlord's fixtures and fittings.

liability insurance

A householder's buildings policy also covers incidents for which you are liable, as owner of the building; for example, if a slate falls off the roof injuring somebody below when the house is empty. If you are the owner-occupier it is the occupier's liability section of your household contents policy (not the buildings policy) that gives cover for claims such as damage or injury caused by the structure of the building: for example, guttering or roof tiles falling, or the branch of a diseased tree in your garden falling on the neighbour's greenhouse and breaking the glass.

wear and tear

Generally excluded from any policy is damage arising from wear and tear (describes 'gradual deterioration') and having neglected to maintain your property. However, where personal liability arises because damage or injury has been caused to other people or their property (such as defective guttering causing dampness in the adjoining house), your insurance policy will cover the damages that could be awarded against you.

For example, you have neglected your house and a slate falls off your roof and damages a passing car, and the rain gets into your roof space. You cannot claim for the cost of repairing the roof and putting right the damage that the rain has caused, because the damage arose from wear and tear. But if your house is sound and it was a storm that blew down the slate, you could claim because storm is an insured peril, and your insurance would also include the water damage.

The insurance will pay compensation to the passing car owner if he makes a claim on you for the damage, irrespective of whether there was a storm causing the tile to fall down, or not. (But he cannot claim on your policy direct.)

If you have neglected to maintain your house, there is the risk that none of these claims would be admissible because there is a question in the proposal form which asks if the property is maintained in a good state of repair. If you answered it wrongly, when taking out the insurance, you would have invalidated the policy. (If you had answered 'no', you would not have got this type of insurance.) A storm claim is often queried by insurers because it may be the result of poor maintenance. Even if your claim gets paid, you may find that you will not get further insurance until the building is safe and sound, or the policy would not be renewed at all because you had lied on the proposal form.

legal expenses insurance

There are some special policies that will pay for legal expenses if a case has to go to court (and will also cover the bill if a case is settled out of court). It covers you for solicitors' bills if you sue somebody, or if you have to defend a case brought against you, but does not cover any compensation you have to pay if you lose the case.

Such a policy would include the legal expenses for a case arising from a dispute with neighbours (about, for example, boundaries, noise, nuisance) but generally building work disputes are excluded.

if in doubt, claim

Every insurance company interprets its policies slightly differently from every other, even if the policies seem similar, so there are no hard and fast rules about claiming – except that fraud would inevitably void any insurance contract.

Policies do vary in what they include in their conditions and exclusions, so when what you think may be a claimable event has happened, get in touch with your insurers (direct or through the broker or agent who got you the policy) and make a claim.

the local authority

Local government as it affects the householder is generally carried out on two levels of responsibility. These are, for most of England and Wales: counties divided into district councils; in Scotland: regions divided into district and island councils; in the main industrial areas of England: metropolitan counties divided into metropolitan district councils; in London: the Greater London Council, divided into London boroughs. The powers of each to make decisions come from acts of parliament and local by-laws.

The main functions of local government relevant to the householder include responsibility for the administration of:

county councils
* refuse disposal (in Wales this is administered by the district councils)
* major roads and road haulage
* planning and development control
* building control (in Inner London)

district councils
* housing
* environmental health (including clean air)
* refuse collection
* minor road maintenance
* planning
* building control (outside Inner London)

elected representatives

The local councillor is the elected local representative responsible for the ward in which you live. He or she is the person to whom to address any problems connected with local authority services, and through whom to make suggestions for improvements, such as providing public skips and bottle-banks.

The extent to which a local councillor can help his constituents may depend on whether he belongs to the ruling party or is a member of an opposition party.

It is the responsibility of the councillors to form policies and for the officers of the council to carry them out, provided that this is within the law.

central government control

The central government's role is that of supervision, finance, and ensuring that the local authorities carry out their functions and duties. Central government provides a large proportion of the finance which is required to top up the revenue raised through rates.

A number of ministerial departments have responsibility for local government. These include the Department of Environment which deals with matters of housing, local government, some aspects of building regulations, construction, planning, environmental pollution.

services provided by the local authority

The local authority is restricted to exercising its powers in its own area. In certain cases there may be an agreement with adjoining authorities, about dealing with sections of land which overlap or where the boundary artificially divides.

rubbish removal

Most local authorities have responsibility for the removal of household refuse. The frequency of collection varies between local authorities; it should be done at regular intervals.

If they fail to maintain the service, the occupier of the premises may 'serve notice' on them; that is, ask that the rubbish be collected. This can be done by phone or going in person, or in writing. If nothing happens in seven days after the notice, you can take action against the local authority in the magistrates' court. The court can impose a fine for every day during which the default continues, but the fine is not paid over to the householder whose rubbish has not been collected.

The local by-laws may require occupiers to do certain things to make the removal of household refuse easier, such as that the dustbins must be placed on the roadside on certain days, or that a particular size of bin must be used.

what is collected

The contents of the dustbin should be household refuse. Strictly speaking, garden rubbish is not part of household refuse and the local authority does not have to remove it – nor anything that is unhygienic or would be a danger to health (such as loose asbestos).

The local authority must remove household refuse without charge, but can make a reasonable charge for the removal of trade refuse. There may be some dispute whether the refuse is of a household or trade. It is the nature of the refuse which determines whether it is household or trade, not the premises from which it comes.

Some local authorities will collect excess rubbish for an agreed fee; usually an inspector will come round to estimate how much it will cost, and tell you what the conditions are (such as that it will have to be in bags).

skips

In some areas, the local authority provides a public skip at regular intervals, for limited periods (which may be as short as one week).

hiring a skip

Skips are hired out by waste disposal service firms and by some local authorities. The skip hirer's name and telephone number must be displayed on the side of a skip, so one way of finding a hiring firm is by looking at other people's skips.

Before deciding on a particular hire firm, make sure that they will supply lights and that the skip will be the right size for your needs. There are mini-skips as well as the ordinary size.

If you are going to leave a skip on the road, you need a permit from your local authority before you can put it there. Some hirers obtain the permit as part of their service, and charge you. The local authority usually needs 5 working days to issue a permit and to notify the local police.

It is your responsibility to make sure that the legal requirements under section 31 of the Highways Act 1971 are complied with. They relate to the siting of the skip, its size, visibility, lighting and removal.

smoke control

Many urban residential areas have been created 'smoke control' areas, under the Clean Air Act. It is an offence for any smoke to be emitted from a building in a smoke control area. It is also an offence to obtain, or to deliver, smoke-producing fuel for use in such an area.

Although you can light a bonfire in the garden in a smoke control area, you must not burn any refuse in an incinerator and must not burn anything other than special 'smokeless' fuels in the house.

If you have to alter or replace your fireplace to avoid contravening a smoke control order, the local authority must repay seven-tenths of reasonable costs of this work.

Installing a new solid fuel boiler in any premises in a smoke control area or smokeless zone requires approval of the public health authority, who must be satisfied that the boiler is an authorised appliance and the flue terminals are appropriately constructed.

Smokeless zones were created by local by-laws before the Clean Air Act came into effect. They place similar restrictions on burning anything other than smokeless fuel.

The National Society for Clean Air, 136 North Street, Brighton BN1 1RG, whose aim is to secure improvements to the environment by the reduction of air pollution, noise and other contaminants, publishes technical papers, books, educational material and a quarterly magazine for specialists and laymen.

highways

A highway (which includes footpaths) is any portion of land over which 'every subject of the crown' may lawfully pass: that is, it must be open to all members of the public, as of right, at all times, not only to a restricted group or only at certain hours. A person has the right to pass over the highway, but does not have a right to stop or stand, sit or stay on it, so that a policeman can lawfully request you to 'move along there, please'.

obstruction of the highway
Where a property directly fronts onto the highway, you have a limited right to obstruct it if you need to have repair work carried out to your property, as long as you avoid unnecessary inconvenience to other road users.

In some areas, a licence has to be obtained from the local authority (and a licence fee paid) for placing skips, scaffolding, site hoardings or building materials on a footpath or road. If there is likely to be scaffolding or other obstructions outside your property for more than one day, contact your local authority and find out if there are any such controls where you live.

upkeep
The local authority must undertake the cleansing of streets and is required, by statute, to keep roads and pavements in a reasonable condition. It may be difficult to determine what standard of maintenance is reasonable: these standards may be flexible. Successful court actions have been brought by road users for injury or damage caused as a direct result of a poorly maintained road surface.

parked cars
The parking of a car is something to which one has no right, although it is generally accepted as a matter of practice.

A householder has right of access to the highway from his property. However, if someone else's car blocks your own drive, you may curse and swear, but must not take retribution on the vehicle; all you can do is to leave a stern note on the windscreen. You would put yourself in the wrong by, for example, letting down his tyres. The police may, in some cases, help by removing the car, but are more likely to – at most – reprimand the returning motorist.

Cars parked on the pavement can cause damage to the paving, and the vehicle owner can be made to pay the cost of replacing any broken paving stones which are directly attributable to the vehicle being placed there.

abandoned cars

You do not have a right to abandon your redundant car, van or other vehicle on the kerbside. If you do and the local authority traces you, you can be fined. The authority is responsible for removing any abandoned car from the highway, subject to a notice having been fixed to the car for a minimum period (which varies between three and seven days). The authority may dispose of the vehicle after a period of storage, unless it is evident right from the start that there is no running life left in the vehicle, in which case it can be sold for scrap straightaway.

If somebody has abandoned a car on your land, you must not damage or dispose of it, but should try to locate the owner. Report it to the police who may be able to trace the owner through the registration number of the vehicle.

adopted and unadopted roads

A street which is fully maintained and repaired by, and at the cost of, the local authority is an adopted road.

A private road (maybe a road leading to a block of flats or running from the block to the garages) is not maintained at the expense of the local authority. The cost of maintenance and repair usually falls on the occupants of the flats, and the money required for this is generally raised through the service charge, or by special levies.

unadopted

In some areas there are unmade, unsurfaced, roads, not adopted by the local authority.

If your property fronts onto such a road, there is a chance that at some stage a decision will be made to carry out substantial works to surface the road. The cost of this may be apportioned among the people in the road, on the basis of the frontage of each property in relation to the total length of the frontages facing the road that is being repaired.

new developments

This does not apply to properties built after 1951 because, since then, the developer or builder is required to deposit (or produce security for) his share of the estimated cost of making up the road to the required standard of the local authority. What happens in new developments is that the developer or builder usually promises to construct the new road to a certain standard, by a certain time. This promise would be no good to the buyer of the property if the builder goes bust. It is therefore important that the builder has made an agreement with the local authority (under the Highways Act 1980) which lays down technical requirements and specifications for the construction of the road, and that the agreement to build the road is supported by a bond or guarantee.

The importance of the bond is that if the builder fails to construct the road properly, or at all, and the local authority have then to do the work, the cost can be recovered from the bondsman (usually a bank). But the local authority generally proceeds against the frontagers to recover the cost of works, not the bondsman, and the frontagers then have to recover from the bondsman. Owners, and new buyers where the road is not made up, should therefore ensure that the builder's bond is sufficient to cover any possible liability.

making up and adopting

The decision to make up a road lies with the local authority. But if the majority of the householders whose frontages face onto a road for more than a hundred yards request the local authority to make up the road, the local authority has to do so.

By adopting the road and taking over responsibility for the maintenance, the local authority will not acquire ownership of the land lying beneath the road surface: the householders will keep the benefit of the land.

Before the local authority will adopt responsibility for the future maintenance of a private road, that road must be in the same condition as if they had constructed it themselves. The responsibility for meeting the cost of getting the road up to that standard will fall on the owners whose properties front onto the road.

The local authority will usually carry out all the works required, and charge the owners of frontages their proportion of the cost. The householder should be supplied with a specification and estimate of the likely cost. The freehold owners of the land which fronts onto the road are liable to pay; this means that in the first instance, no tenants are likely to be affected. When their rent is reviewed, they may be asked for a contribution: the value of their property may have been improved by the better quality of the road access.

The financial burden on the freeholders can be substantial, and many local authorities will accept payments to be made in instalments over a number of years.

Although the cost is distributed on the basis of frontages, sometimes contributions will be required in excess of the amount directly based on the calculation of a frontage. This would be where a property is set to the rear of land fronting onto the road, and is approached by a driveway or path. The frontage to the street may merely be the width of the access road, and using this as the basis of the calculation would be unfair to other frontage owners and road users. The calculations are then usually a matter of discussion, argument, and compromise.

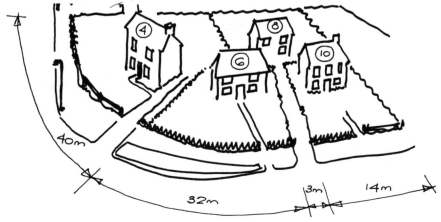

sewerage

The local authority is responsible for providing and maintaining sewers, as agents for the regional water authority (or, in a few areas, local water company).

Of the two types of sewer (public and private) the public sewer belongs to the authority, which is responsible for providing such sewers as are – and will be – necessary for effectively draining the district, and also for the sewage works.

The local authority is empowered to construct sewers in any street or in any private land, after giving reasonable notice to the owner or occupier of the land. It must pay compensation for any loss which the owner or occupier may suffer as a result of the construction.

If a new sewer is constructed where previously none existed, the local authority can recover the cost from properties with a frontage to the street in which the sewer is constructed.

The owner or occupier of any premises is entitled, as a right, to have the private sewer (drain) connected to the public sewer.

It is illegal to empty into any public sewer, or any drain communicating with a public sewer, anything prejudicial to health, or anything likely to cause damage to the sewer or drain, such as chemical refuse or petroleum spirit.

The local authority is empowered to take action where there are problems or defects such as

* where the drainage is not satisfactory, or none at all has been provided
* where a cesspool, private sewer, soil pipe, rainwater pipe, is insufficient, or a private sewer is so defective as to admit subsoil water and discharge it into a public sewer
* where any of the drainage appliances in a property are in such a condition as to be a danger to health or to cause nuisance (this would include the right to action where a defective rainwater pipe is causing nuisance to an adjoining property).

The local authority, as agent of the water authority, will give notice to the owner of the building requesting him to provide satisfactory drainage, or to do such works as may be necessary – in some circumstances, within 48 hours. If the notice is not complied with, the local authority may carry out the work themselves, and recover the cost from the person on whom the notice was served.

cesspools and septic tanks

Cesspools are effectively tanks which store the effluent drained from the property, generally in areas where the public sewer is too far away. Cesspools have no outlets and should be watertight; they require to be emptied frequently.

The cost of emptying cesspools is passed on to the householder by the relevant authority who carries out this work.

Septic tanks (much more common than cesspools) are also used in areas remote from public sewers. They require to be emptied at intervals of, say, one year or longer. Most water authorities provide this service. If not, a private contractor has to be engaged.

If your house is not connected to the public sewer but served by a cesspool or septic tank, make sure that the water bill does not include a charge for sewerage.

getting a grant

Local authorities have a duty (under various Housing Acts) to make available grants for carrying out improvements, renovation and repairs to property. The way in which this duty is interpreted varies.

The purpose of grants is to maintain existing housing: the grants are given to the properties rather than to the persons who may occupy or own the buildings. The individual circumstances of the applicant are largely ignored, except in cases of hardship or where the person is registered as handicapped.

There are four types of grants: improvement, intermediate, repairs and special.

improvement grant

Improvement grants are intended for major improvements to help bring homes built before 1961 to a good standard. So, improvements to modern houses or fully equipped houses in good repair would not qualify. These grants are also given in order to provide more homes by converting existing property into several housing units – but not simply for enlarging a house to provide more bedroom space.

The property must be capable of being improved to a good condition, and you may be required to improve existing amenities and poor layout arrangements, such as a bathroom that has to be approached through another room, or a w.c. directly off the kitchen.

A tenant can apply for an improvement grant subject to the landlord's consent having been given. An owner-occupier will be eligible for an improvement grant only if the rateable value of the property is not more than £225 (in London, £400; in Scotland, £335). However, these limits do not apply if the grant is needed to improve a home for a disabled person, or if the property is in a housing action area. To find out if yours is, ask the housing department or the environmental health department of your local authority.

It is rare for an application for an improvement grant to be accepted if it is for less than £1,000 of work.

The improvement grant is based on a maximum eligible expenditure of £6,600 (in London, £9,000). For priority cases, where standard amenities are missing, the maximum eligible expenditure is £10,200 (in London and in Scotland, £13,800). The maximum grant which can be given is currently 75% of the total cost. This is available for each unit of occupation which is created, so that where five flats are being created, the eligible grant would be available for each unit.

An improvement grant is discretionary and the decision rests with the local authority.

intermediate grant

Such a grant is made to help meet the cost of improving pre-1961 homes by putting in missing standard amenities, such as bath, shower, washbasin, sink, hot and cold water supply, an inside w.c. Associated with this sort of grant may be repairs to the property. The council may require you to put the whole house or flat into reasonable repair.

The maximum eligible expenditure for an intermediate grant is £3,000 (in London, £4,200). If repairs and replacements are carried out at the same time, the maximum eligible expenditure for the repairs element of an intermediate grant is £2,275 (in London, £3,005). It is possible to claim a smaller amount for minor repairs. The maximum total comes to £5,275 (in London, £7,205); 75% of this maximum cost is what can be given as this grant.

Intermediate grants are mandatory: the local authority must give you an intermediate grant if satisfied that you meet the basic requirements.

repairs grant

These grants are made for carrying out substantial or structural repairs to homes built before 1919 with a rateable value of not more than £225 (in London, £400). If the house or flat needs major repairs and you are not eligible for an improvement grant, you may be able to get a repairs grant. Anyone getting an intermediate grant cannot also get a repairs grant for the same property.

To qualify for a repairs grant, the work to be done must be a major structural repair – for example, work to the roof, walls, floors or foundations. Routine maintenance work, such as rewiring or the replacement of worn fixtures does not qualify for a repairs grant. It is essential that all repairs that are going to be required are included, because it is a once-and-for-all grant and there is no provision for an annual top-up.

A major item which is usually included in a repairs grant is a new roof, which includes gutters and downpipes. The roof structure has to be adequate to support the weight of the proposed new covering, and the cost of repair or strengthening the roof timbers is included in the repairs grant.

Windows may be included as an item in a repairs grant. There is no point in applying if just one window frame requires replacement: this in itself would not be a justified claim. But if half or more of the windows in the house or flat need repairing, a claim may be made.

Where a grant is requested for roof or windows, the remainder of the property must be capable of being brought up to a requisite standard. If the quality of, for example, pointing, or a damp-proof course, is not up to standard, repairs will be required to be made before the grant is given. The property must be able to satisfy an anticipated life of 15–30 years.

These grants are at the discretion of the local authority, and in many parts of the country they are currently not available. For example, many London boroughs have announced as a matter of policy that there will be no repairs grants for owner-occupied property in 1984/5.

The maximum eligible expenditure is £4,800 (in London, £6,600); the maximum percentage grant is 75%. Higher limits apply to buildings which are listed as being of special architectural or historic interest.

If an earlier grant has been made to the property, this may influence any new application. Repairs grants are not paid on houses which have previously received an improvement grant. Only in exceptional circumstances will a repairs grant be considered for a property which has had a previous grant. And even then it only means that the local authority would look at the situation: there is no guarantee that the repairs grant would be forthcoming.

special grant

Special grants are for basic improvements to amenities and for providing means of escape from fire in a house in multiple occupation in which tenants share facilities.

A tenant is not eligible for a special grant, only the landlord – that is the owner of the property; for a leaseholder, there must be at least 5 years of lease to run.

Maximum eligible expenditure is £8,100 (in London, £10,800). The maximum grant is 75% of cost.

Such grants are normally discretionary. But if the council has served notice requiring work of this kind to be carried out, a special grant will be given, at the maximum specified rate.

disabled grant

While the maximum of any of the four grants is 75% of cost, if an applicant is registered with the Department of Health and Social Security and classified as disabled, he may be able to get from the DHSS half of the 25% difference. This means that only 12.5% of the cost has to be provided by the applicant.

'Disabled' grants are not once-and-for-all if an ailment is progressive, and future applications can include repair work as well as new work. Each application is dealt with entirely on its merit. No disabled grant is paid for work under £500.

loans

Many local authorities provide loans to cover the gap between the grant and the total cost of the work. In order to qualify, the applicant must first have tried to get a loan by way of an extension of his existing mortgage and been refused. The local authority may take a second mortgage on the property, if it is freehold or has a minimum of ten years left on the lease. The borrower would have to show that he is capable of meeting the repayments plus interest on the loans, at approximately 3% above the banks' base lending rate.

Pensioners may be able to get a maturity loan, where the capital has to be repaid on death (or when the property changes hands), and only the interest on the loan has to be paid.

insulation

A separate grant is available towards the cost of insulating roof spaces and lagging tanks and pipes in a house with inadequate loft insulation (that is, less than 30 mm) or with no existing loft insulation. For someone who is elderly or disabled on a low income the grant is 90% up to a maximum of £95; for everyone else it is 66%, up to a maximum of £69.

before and after ownership

When you buy a house or flat, it is possible to make an application before you own the property, but such an application will not be approved prior to completion.

Getting a grant does not absolve you from obtaining planning permission where necessary, nor from complying with the Building Regulations.

An owner-occupier who sells to another owner-occupier does not have to repay the grant, but if a landlord or developer wants to sell on within a specified time (generally 5 years), he must repay all or part of the grant, with interest (but not in Scotland).

how to apply for a grant

● Find out from the local authority whether a grant has been paid for that property (phone or write, giving the full address, or go in person)
● if you are going to use a surveyor or architect, get him to help complete the application form for your local authority and to supply the drawings (reasonable fees of professional advisers – such as surveyor or architect – are in themselves grant-aidable)
● decide which of the four available grants you are more likely to be eligible for
● put in the application together with preliminary details, as soon as possible; further details such as building quotes, costs, and drawings can be submitted at a later date.

If you do not hear from the local authority check after about 6 weeks, and at regular intervals thereafter, to find out if – and when – your application is accepted. There may be a long queue for grants and a long delay before your application is granted. In the meantime, building costs may have gone up. You may want to update the quotation to make sure that the grant is realistic for the prices at the time. Once the grant is confirmed, you cannot change any part of the application.

information required for an application

● Address of property to be improved or converted; whether it was built, improved, or converted before October 1961
● full name of applicant; if joint owners (for example a husband and wife), both names must be inserted
● day-time telephone number and the address
● if a disabled person is making the application for an improvement grant, this should be stated

- land tenure: freeholder, or holder of a lease with x years to run, or tenant; tenant includes:
  - a regulated tenant of a private landlord or an unregistered housing association, or
  - a tenant with a long tenancy at a low rent which has less than five years to run, or
  - a protected occupier or statutory tenant under the Rent (Agriculture) Act 1976

  a tenant has to set out the full tenancy details and give the name and address of the landlord and a letter stating that he approves of the work which is to be carried out

- rateable value of the property
- if the property is mortgaged, name and address of the mortgagee (building society, bank etc.) and account number
- description of the work to be done; something simple will do, such as 'renovation' or 'extension'
- whether planning permission and Building Regulations approval are required and, if an application for them has been made, whether either has been refused (if either has been refused, there is no point in proceeding with an application for a grant).

Most forms have a space for 'firm's name and address' to be stated on it (i.e. architect, surveyor). If all communications go via the address of the surveyor or architect acting for you, you will have to meet the firm's fees for this, too.

- name for the payment of grant: if a bridging loan has been obtained, it may be necessary to insert the name of the bank (builder's name may be inserted if this is part of his agreement and in his contract); generally, it is unwise to have the money paid to anyone other than directly to yourself.

For an application for a repairs grant, further information is required:

- was the property built before 1 January 1919?
- is the application made as the result of receiving a notice under Section 9 of the Housing Act 1957 (such a notice is served where a

house is in dire disrepair and, if so, the grant becomes mandatory).

For an improvement or an intermediate grant, you have to state the standard amenities which are to be provided: a fixed bath or shower for example, or a sink with a hot and cold water supply, or a w.c.

You are asked whether the amenities to be provided have been missing for at least twelve months, whether they will be for the exclusive use of the occupants of the dwelling, and whether they are needed for a disabled person.

The completed forms should be signed as being correct: you would be committing fraud if you deliberately miscompleted the form.

You will have to submit the following:

* plans of the property prior to alteration
* plans of the property after the work has been carried out
* specification of the works, itemised with costs to each item (including VAT); costs of decoration are not to be included except when they are justified by replacement or repairs.

after the application

If there is a long delay between the time of the estimate and the work being done, the estimate may be adjusted at any stage up to its formal approval – for example, if the builder has to adjust the figures to take account of increases in costs. But once it has been approved, it cannot be varied either up or down.

Work should not start before you get written approval of your application. (This may be many months later.) The cost of any work done before approval does not qualify for a grant. When your application has been approved, the work must be started within one year.

You remain responsible for all the costs incurred during building construction and must make your own provisions for any delays in getting grant payments. But an application for an interim payment may be made during the course of the work. Where unforeseen items occur during work, an application can be made for an additional amount, provided that the maximum grant has not already been given.

Eventually, when the work for which the grant was given is completed, the local authority surveyor (in London, the district surveyor) will come to inspect the work that has been done and must approve it before the grant is paid.

Most local authorities give the applicants the option of having the grant paid directly to them, or to their builder, or to their architect or surveyor. In some cases, it can be made payable directly to the bank if short-term finance has been provided for the work to proceed before the grant money is available.

not getting a grant

The decision of the local authority is final and is not open to discussion or query.

Grants which are at the discretion of the local authority could be suspended if the local authority does not have enough money. At present, the government is cutting down on these grants – some councils are still encouraging applications, others are not able to cope with demands.

When a discretionary grant is not approved, the council does not have to enter into correspondence with the public.

Building Regulations approval

Before carrying out alterations to a property, you may need planning consent and will probably need Building Regulations approval.

Building Regulations

The purpose of the Building Regulations is to ensure that the way a house is built or altered is reasonably durable, with a moderate life expectancy, and unlikely to cause any injury to the health, life or limbs of the occupants or passers-by. In essence, they attempt to control the method used for the construction, rather than the appearance of the building.

The regulations deal with such matters as the fitness of materials to be used; preparations of the site, protection of walls, the prevention of damp, weather resistance; structural fire precautions, thermal and sound insulations; the size of windows and the open space required outside them, the means of ventilation, the height of rooms; drainage and private sewers.

You should get Building Regulations approval from the local authority before starting any building work, structural alterations or extensions to an existing building. Notice of intention to build, and drawings, should be submitted to the local authority before work starts.

Where a building is being altered or improved, the regulations will apply not only to the part which is being dealt with but can become relevant to the remainder of the building. This means, for example, that if you extend your two-storey property by providing an extra floor with habitable rooms (not just a loft conversion), the whole of the property may become subject to special fire regulations, and require self-closing fireproof doors.

Some alterations may therefore involve extra expenditure, which you had not anticipated.

General repairs and maintenance do not need Building Regulations approval so long as no structural work is involved.

applying

An application for Building Regulations approval requires two copies of the formal notification and the requisite number of drawings.

Most authorities issue guidance notes about the information required from the drawings, as well as information and guidance on filling in the relevant forms.

The forms are available from the administrative offices of the local authority. You can phone the local town hall and ask to be put through to the building control officer and ask for the forms to be sent to you.

The drawings have to show details of the materials which are to be used and the method of construction. The appearance of the building alterations is not relevant, only the technical methods intended to be used. It is essential that the method of construction meets the requirements set out in the relevant regulations. A complicated amount of information has to go into a drawing to meet all the relevant controls.

the building inspector

If you wish to carry out alterations to your property, it is wise to contact the building inspector for your area, and arrange to go and see him with your proposals.

If the local inspector is consulted at a very early stage, he may give you some advice and help in putting the relevant information onto the drawings. But his duty is to check the drawings when submitted, not to produce them. In some areas, building inspectors are reluctant to examine proposals and will insist on an application having been made before they will discuss your plans.

The building inspector is responsible to the present and future occupiers of the premises for the standard of work, so that the building will be safe and sound now and in the future. He may, therefore, inspect the work at every stage, as it progresses.

fees

A plan fee and an inspection fee have to be paid for an application. If you are eligible for an improvement or intermediate grant, you can normally recoup a percentage of the fee.

Fees are payable in two stages: plan fees on application for approval of the building plans, and an inspection fee following the first inspection of works on the site. If the local authority fails to approve, or if it rejects, the application, the application fee will not be refunded but a site inspection charge will not be payable because there will be no inspection.

Should the application be rejected and re-submitted with amendments at a later date, a second application charge will not be made, provided it is essentially the same project.

If the local authority chooses not to inspect, the inspection fee will not be charged.

The fees for England and Wales are set out in the Building (Prescribed Fees) (Amendments) Regulations 1983, according to the type of work, namely fees payable for extensions and alterations:

	plan fee	inspection fee
★ porch more than 2 square metres but not exceeding 4 square metres	£3	£9
★ porch more than 4 square metres but not exceeding 20 square metres	£7	£19
★ providing one or more rooms in roof space and access to them	£13	£39
★ any other extension not exceeding 20 square metres	£7	£19
★ any other extension more than 20 square metres but not exceeding 40 square metres	£13	£39

for other work to existing houses, the fee is based on 70% of the estimated building cost, for example

cost under £1,000, plan fee £3 and inspection fee £9
cost £1,000 and under £2,000, plan fee £7 and inspection fee £21
cost £2,000 and under £3,000, plan fee £9 and inspection fee £27
cost £5,000 and under £6,000, plan fee £18 and inspection fee £54
cost £9,000 and under £10,000, plan fee £29 and inspection fee £87
cost £20,000 and under £25,000, plan fee £57 and inspection fee £171
cost £40,000 and under £45,000, plan fee £95 and inspection fee £285.

You, as the applicant are responsible for the fees; the contractor or builder generally makes the payment and adds the cost to your bill, including VAT.

professional fees
If you engage an architect or chartered surveyor, his charge for preparing the drawings and completing the forms should be part of his total fee.

Where the proposed alterations involve redesign of retaining walls or special foundations (if difficult ground conditions are involved), you may have to get an engineer to provide the drawings and calculations for submission to the building inspector. For small works, most engineers charge on an hourly rate in the region of £25, plus VAT, costs and disbursements.

approval

You should hear from the local authority within five weeks of the date of application (or two months, by agreement) whether your plans have been approved or rejected. If you do not hear within that time, they have not been approved.

Building Regulations approval can only be withheld if the proposed work as set out in the drawings does not comply with one or more of the regulations – irrespective of how trivial such a contravention may be. It is a technical application and is not subject to the judgment of a committee, as can happen with a planning application.

notice of commencement

A builder has to provide the local authority with at least 24 hours notice, in writing, of the date and time when he will start building operations, and must also notify the local authority when various stages of construction have been or are about to be completed.

If no notice is given, the local authority may require the builder to open up the construction so that the inspector may see how it was built and check that the regulations have not been contravened.

If he is not satisfied, he may require you to rebuild in a manner which meets his approval. If this is not done, the local authority can then alter the work themselves, and charge the owner of the building with the cost.

contravening the Building Regulations

It is an offence to carry out work which does not meet the requirements of the Building Regulations. If you do not get approval, or start work before approval is granted and the work does not comply with the regulations, the local authority can ask you to pull the work down and alter it so that it will meet the regulations or, if you do not do this, they can (after 28 days) alter it and charge you for it.

You can also be fined a maximum of £100 for each regulation contravened (there are 161 altogether), with an extra £10 for each day after conviction that you do not put the work right. The same applies if the plans have been approved, but the work itself contravenes the regulations.

in Scotland

The Building Regulations operate throughout England and Wales (except Inner London). In Scotland, building control is regulated by the Building Standard (Scotland) Regulations 1981.

The local authority's approval is called a building warrant. Fees for warrants are based on the estimated cost of the operations and should accompany the application.

Work can proceed when a warrant has been issued (normally within fourteen days), but notice is required in writing of the date on which work is started. Within 14 days of completion, if the work is satisfactory, the authority will issue a certificate.

Inner London

The Building Regulations do not cover buildings in the Inner London area. Inner London is the area which was under the control of the London County Council before the Greater London Council (GLC) was formed in 1965. Planning in Inner London is controlled by the same legislation as England and Wales, but building in the Inner London area is subject to the London Building Acts and the London Building (Constructional) By-laws 1972 to 1979.

The following boroughs are in Inner London:
Camden
City
Greenwich
Hackey
Hammersmith and Fulham
Islington
Kensington and Chelsea
Lambeth
Lewisham
Southwark
Tower Hamlets
Wandsworth
Westminster

If you are in doubt whether your area is effectively Inner London, look in the telephone directory under 'Greater London Council' for the district surveyor's number, listed under Architect's Department. Telephone the district surveyor's office nearest to you, and ask whether your particular address falls within his zone of control.

no formal approval required

Inner London building law is different in a number of ways. Some aspects of building work (such as thermal and sound insulation) are not controlled; on the other hand, there is more rigorous control over, for example, means of escape measures in case of fire.

Formal approval of plans is not required before work starts. Instead, the builder has the responsibility of informing the district surveyor at least two days before work begins, by means of a building notice form (obtainable from the district surveyor's office), and the district surveyor will respond only if the proposals are unacceptable. It is, however, sensible in the majority of cases to discuss your proposals in advance with the district surveyor. He may well ask the builder for plans and technical information after he has received his notification, so that he can inspect the work properly on site as it proceeds.

fees in London

Because there is no requirement for formal approval of plans in Inner London, building control fees are payable only when the district surveyor has completed his inspection and the building work is completed. The scale of fees is related to the cost of the work, as follows:

	£
cost is £100 or less	10.00
cost is over £100, up to £1,000	10.00
plus for every £100 (or part of £100) by which the cost exceeds £100	2.25
cost is over £1,000, up to £5,000	30.25
plus for every £100 (or part of £100) by which the cost exceeds £1,000	.75
cost is over £5,000, up to £1,000,000	60.25
plus for every £100 (or part of £100) by which the cost exceeds £5,000	.45

In the first instance, the builder is liable for the fee, but if he fails to pay it, the account becomes the liability of the owner of the property.

planning permission

Before 1949, there was no national system of planning control over the appearance of new buildings or the extent of any alterations to existing ones.

Planning permission is now required for any action which may be referred to as 'development'.

what is development?

Development includes making any material change in the use of any building or other land.

Excluded from the definition of development is maintenance, improvement, or other alterations to the building which affect only the inside of the property, not the external appearance.

'permitted development'

You can carry out a substantial number of alterations to your property which do not require an application for planning permission, as long as they are internal changes which do not affect the exterior or alter the existing use of the building, such as removing a partition between a front room and a rear room, or even converting two houses into one. But you do need planning permission if you want to convert an existing property into flats, because that effectively changes the use from a single family dwelling to multiple occupation.

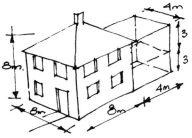

Volume of House
8 × 8 × 8 = 512 cubic meters
MAXIMUM EXTENSION FOR A
DETACHED ENGLISH HOUSE
70 cubic meters or 15%
of volume up to MAX 115 m³
PROPOSED EXTENSION ✓ YES
4 × 4 × 3 = 48 m³. ✓ YES
2 floors = 96 m³. ✗ NO
because 15% of 512 m³ is 76.8 m³.

You do not need planning permission to enlarge your home if no previous extension or enlargement has taken place and the proposed development does not affect the front of the building, or any part that is visible from the street. The enlargement for a terraced house must not exceed 50 cubic metres, or one-tenth of the existing volume of the building, up to a maximum extension of 115 cubic metres. For a detached house, it must not be more than 70 cubic metres in England or Wales, or 15% of the volume (50 cubic metres or 20% of the volume in Scotland).

This means that, in most cases, an extra room at the back on the ground floor does not require planning permission nor does creating rooms in a loft, or putting in dormer windows overlooking the rear garden.

You can erect or construct a porch outside your house without planning permission, so long as the floor area of the porch is not more than 2 sq metres, and the height not more than 3 metres, and no part of the porch gets nearer than 2 metres from the front boundary where it joins the street or highway.

A garden shed or a greenhouse may be erected within your property, provided that they are not at the front of your building, and are not higher than three metres (4 metres if a ridged roof) and not bigger in floor area than half of the existing ground area of your garden, excluding the area of house.

It is not just size and site that matter, but also use. You can put up a shed in your back garden, half the size of your ground floor, but if you use it as a garage (or a stable), planning permission would generally have to be obtained. And if you intended to live there, that would be regarded as creating a new dwelling, and would need planning permission.

You can put up a gate, fence, wall or other enclosure to the front of your property provided it is not more than one metre in height. The remainder of your property you may enclose with fences up to a maximum height of two metres.

Trees, shrubs, and bushes are not subject to planning control. There is little to prevent you from growing a hedge of enormous proportions, but the local authority can control the brick wall round a garden or the height of a palisade fence.

There is a chance that a neighbour will complain when you start making alterations to your property. It is wise to have discussed your proposal with the planning authority, and to have sent them a copy of your proposals, so that they have it on record that you will be carrying out work for which planning permission is not required. This should avoid the need for a dispute with anyone at the local planning authority who is not aware of your proposals but is only too well aware of the complaints that he has received about what you propose to do.

when planning permission is needed

New buildings, major alterations, enlargements of an existing building and many changes in the use of a building or land need planning permission. The local authority have the right and duty to control these changes. 'Control' ranges from preventing the increase of noise, pollution and traffic congestion, to minimising the loss of good farmland, and means finding a balance between the need for change and the wish of most people to see the countryside and the character of their neighbourhood unchanged.

who decides planning applications

A planning application is submitted to a planning officer for the local authority. He or his staff will inspect the proposals, check the drawings and produce a report. In many areas, the decision for small applications is delegated to the planning officer.

The remainder of the applications will be submitted to a planning committee who will decide, based on the planning officer's report, whether to reject or approve your proposal.

The planning committee is made up from the elected members of the local authority who are a lay panel and do not necessarily have any planning expertise.

The planning committee will consider the appearance of your proposed alteration and its effect on other householders and properties nearby. The committee's reaction to your proposals may be based on their own views of what is an acceptable appearance, and how much change to allow.

They will not automatically protect rights of light, where a proposed new development might interfere with the amount of daylight to adjoining properties. But they will consider privacy, for example, to what extent a neighbour's property would be overlooked as a result of the alteration. (For this reason, an application may not be granted for the conversion of a flat roof to a balcony or patio, or one which includes a large side window in an extension.)

Discussing your proposals with the planning officers before making an application may save you drawing up a scheme that will not be accepted. You have to pay for an application for planning permission, so you might as well get it right. If you have been to see the planning officer and discussed your proposals, it is likely that the application will be dealt with more smoothly and quickly.

the official procedure

To make an application for planning permission you have to fill in form M (TP1), available from the town hall (generally, four copies of the completed form are required). On this form, apart from informing the planning authority about your proposals, you have to indicate your ownership of or involvement with the property. There is nothing to stop you making an application for a property or piece of land which you do not own, provided that the requisite notice is given to the owner of the land.

Planning permission is simply what the words imply. It does not mean that it is inevitably practicable to construct the building on the site for which the consent has been granted. It is quite possible to get planning permission and still be left with structural or ownership obstacles.

drawings with application for planning permission

An application for planning permission requires a site plan showing the relationship of the property to the street and its neighbours. (An extract from the ordnance survey map of the area is acceptable for this.) It also requires drawings showing the external elevations of the property and the proposed alterations to the appearance of the building clearly marked on them. It is usual to provide scale drawings of each of the external walls and roof of the property.

For proposed internal alterations to the property, you will also have to submit plans, to scale, representing what you would see if the building were cut horizontally at a height of approximately 1.2 metres above each floor. This horizontal cut goes through the windows and door openings, cupboards and staircases and shows the arrangements of the accommodation in the building.

It is important that the officers and lay members of the planning committee should be able to understand what you propose to do to your property, through the drawings which are submitted. If they are left in doubt, they may reject an application. Planning applications incur fees, paid to the local authority, so make sure that the drawings are sufficiently explicit for the planning committee.

The fees are £24 for an application in relation to any work to an existing house or in the garden, £47 for any other application – for example, a new building such as a garage.

response to applications

Local planning authorities are required to deal with a planning application within eight weeks from the date of submission, unless the applicant agrees in writing to a longer period. There could be a delay beyond the eight week period if you are requested to provide further information on, or amendments to, your proposals.

Your application may be approved subject to certain conditions. For example, the local authority may insist that the materials to be used for an extension to a house must match the existing materials; or they may place a restriction on the use of land or a building.

The planning authority can take enforcement proceedings against you if you fail to comply with the conditions. You have the right to appeal against conditions – but this would open the entire matter of your application for planning permission to review by the Secretary of State.

refusal and appeal

If permission is refused, the notice you get should list the reasons, and you have the right to appeal against the refusal to the Secretary of State. This must be done within six months. Do not hesitate to ask the planning officer for advice on the appeal procedures (which could be by public enquiry or by both sides making written representations).

There is no fee for making an appeal, but professional planning advice may have to be paid for. The Royal Town Planning Institute can advise you about obtaining the services of a planning consultant and in certain cases voluntary planning aid is available.

Amongst the Institute's free leaflets, available from the RTPI, 26 Portland Place, London W1N 4BE, the one entitled *Should I appeal?* sets out details.

if carrying out building work without planning permission

If you start work without planning permission, no fine or penalty is incurred until the local authority advise you that planning permission is required for the development you are carrying out (or have completed in the past). It is often extremely difficult for the local authority to prove that an unauthorised development has taken place: if an extra wing has been added to the back of a building, there may be no record of the appearance of the rear of the property to confirm that an alteration has taken place.

The local authority can enforce planning control generally

* where development has been carried out without planning permission
* where the conditions or limitations which were part of the planning permission have not been fulfilled.

The initial step open to the local planning authority is to serve an enforcement notice. The Town and Country Planning Act 1971 confers the power – but does not impose a duty – to do so, and the authority is not bound always to serve an enforcement notice in every case. However, it must investigate the circumstances if they are brought to its attention.

Generally an enforcement notice can only be served within four years following the date of the breach.

enforcement notice

An enforcement notice must be served on the owner *and* on the occupier of the building to which it relates, and on any other person having an interest in the land. It must specify the matters alleged to constitute a planning breach and the steps the planning authority want to be taken to remedy the breach, and the date by which this must be done. The local authority may require you either to get the necessary planning permission or to restore the property to the state it was in before the development took place.

If the enforcement notice is not complied with, the local planning authority has a number of courses of action open to it. It can, but rarely does, enter your property and carry out whatever the notice demands. For instance, it can order the demolition of a building which has been built without planning consent. (But if the notice required the discontinuance of a use, they cannot, for instance, enter to stop somebody using a shop as a restuarant.)

The local authority coming in, carrying out the work and charging the owner of the building can be a serious matter: if you cannot pay, they are in the same position as a mortgagee and can sell the house to recoup the outstanding cost, irrespective of who currently owns the building.

appeal against an enforcement notice
You have a right of appeal to the Secretary of State for the Environment against an enforcement notice on any of a number of grounds, including:

● that planning permission ought to be granted for the development to which the notice relates or that the condition or limitation that has not been complied with ought to be discharged
● that the matters alleged in the notice do not constitute a breach of planning control
● that the steps required by the notice ask for more to be done than is necessary for putting right any breach of planning control
● that not enough time is allowed for complying.

When an appeal is made, the enforcement notice is suspended until the Secretary of State has given his decision, or the appeal is withdrawn.

The Secretary of State must hold a public enquiry into an appeal if either the local planning authority or the applicant requests it. In all other cases, the matter is dealt with by written depositions.

If you lose the appeal, the council can prosecute you for non-compliance and you would incur a fine for each day that the offending alteration remains.

If planning consent is granted after an appeal against an enforcement notice, the enforcement notice ceases to have an effect, and you can keep the 'offending' building or continue what has been the unauthorised use of the land.

stop notice
The local planning authority can serve a stop notice to stop work being carried out on a building.

A stop notice really means 'stop' and immediately brings to a halt building work on a site. But it cannot be used to prevent the continuance of a use, for example the use of land as a site for a caravan, or for anyone to use the caravan as a main residence. Nor can a stop notice be used for any activity that has been taking place for more than twelve months.

There is no appeal against a stop notice, and it stands or falls with the enforcement notice to which it is related. If the enforcement notice is not substantiated, the local planning authority may be liable to pay compensation for any financial loss which the owner of the property (or, for example, the builders) suffered as a result of the stop notice.

Because of this liability to pay compensation, the stop notice, which is the only short cut available to the local authority, is very rarely used.

listed buildings

Under the town and country planning legislation, many local authorities have drawn up lists of buildings of special architectural or historic interest in their area. They may also have designated conservation areas – perhaps a whole town or village, or a square, a street or even part of a street. Any property in these categories must not be demolished, and a listed building must not be altered or extended in any way which would affect its character without authorisation from the local authority. This is a requirement in addition to any necessary planning permission.

You can check whether a house is in a conservation area or is a listed building, by going to the local authority offices to inspect the list.

what must not be done
It is an offence to demolish or carry out operations affecting the character of a listed building without listed building consent. The local planning authority can serve a listed building enforcement notice, which requires the building to be restored to its former state, or to be brought into the condition it would have been in if the terms

and conditions of any listed building consent had been complied with.

No alteration or extension works may be carried out unless they are authorised by written consent from the local planning authority or the Secretary of State.

Works which are permitted development in non-listed buildings (such as the construction of a porch, or alterations which do not affect the exterior) are not permitted, and listed building consent is required even when planning permission is not.

preservation notice

If a local planning authority think that a building which is not listed is to be altered in such a way as to affect its character, they can serve a building preservation notice, stating that the building appears to them to be of special architectural and historical interest. This notice comes into force immediately, and remains in force for six months, during which time the Secretary of State will decide whether the building should be included in his list.

If you think that your house is a property which should be listed notify the local planning authority of your opinion.

planning permission for development

Planning permission is required for anything which may be referred to as development. Development includes making any significant change in the use of any building or other land.

changes of planning use

Planning permission is required for a change from one planning use to another. The uses to which buildings may be put are divided into a number of categories:

* shop, office, industrial, special industrial, storage;
* hotel, school, religious use, health and welfare, residential institutional (for example, a house for the care of children or old people);
* public and community uses (such as art galleries, museums, public libraries, theatres, cinemas, concert halls);
* dance hall, skating rink, swimming baths, gymnasium and sports hall.

A private home does not fall into any of these categories, but if you change the use of part of your own property from a house you live in into a place of work, you may require planning permission. The test is the extent of the change which has taken place.

If you decide to earn a little money by doing some work from home, current planning law is sufficiently vague to give you no clear rules about the amount you may safely do without needing planning permission. Rules there are, but how they are interpreted and enforced varies.

earning money at home

The use of part of your home for a workshop for something which is mainly a hobby, but which enables you to earn some extra money, is probably not going to be development. If the practising of your hobby begins to cause inconvenience to adjoining householders, it is possible that it may be regarded as development. The use of that same space as an area where you practice your sole employment, and where the money you earn is the majority of your income, is almost certainly development and planning permission is likely to be required.

The use of a garage for storing trade goods other than on a short term temporary basis, requires planning permission.

The crucial point is the extent to which you are using your property for purposes other than as a home for you and your family. Here are some examples.

motor car sales

To supplement your income by selling three or four cars a year may not be regarded as a significant form of development, particularly where nothing takes place which would be evident to a passer-by or disturb the neighbours. But the sale of three or four cars per month would become a significant development, and planning permission would be required. It is highly unlikely that such permission would be given for a home in a quiet residential area, because of the inconvenience caused to the occupants of other houses in the neighbourhood.

The repair or maintenance of motor cars may also cause problems. It is the number of cars worked on which affects the decision: repairing something like 40 cars a year would be significant development, and need planning permission.

Keeping private cars on your property does not require permission, even if several members of the family park their cars in your drive and repair them there. Parking a trade van or even a small lorry on your property in between using it for trips to and from work is acceptable, but anything more would be outside the scope of 'the enjoyment of the dwelling house' and count as development.

caravans

It is not development to park a caravan within the grounds of a house, unless it is used as a separate self-contained unit or by someone who is not a member of the household (for example, rented out as holiday accommodation).

paying guests

Offering bed and breakfast accommodation in the holiday season, or accommodation for students during term-time, may require planning permission if the extent of each constitutes a significant change of use.

The sub-division of a house into two or more separate homes requires planning permission, if it is your intention to create a separate unit. Even if each unit does not have its own bathroom and toilet facilities, as long as it has its own cooking facilities, planning permission will be required. Where groups of people share the house or flat that was previously used by one family and take their meals together, it is not development and will not require planning permission.

When a person pays for his accommodation which he can lock and does his own cleaning and cooking, the property is likely to be referred to as being in multiple paying occupation. This constitutes development and requires planning permission.

professional use

Planning control seems to be lenient about the business use of one's residence for professional purposes. A doctor or dentist does not need planning permission to have a consulting room in his home. However, this does not extend beyond the resident: the use of another room in the house by another dental surgeon constitutes development. Planning permission would also be needed if, for example, a vet wants to use two rooms of his house as a veterinary surgery where he employs a couple of assistants.

In each case, the question is whether the use to which part of the premises has been put is incidental to the main use of the building as a residential dwelling, and the extent of the different use. Using part of one's home as an office may need permission, but teaching music, marking a publisher's proofs, part-time hairdressing, have all been decided as not needing planning permission.

It would appear that planning permission is not needed to carry out a business in one's own home provided that there are no employees and no-one visits the home in a way that would cause disturbance to the neighbours.

People who use their property as they wish and make sure that they minimise any inconvenience to neighbours, and that to the casual observer there is no outward appearance of a business being carried on, probably will not need to get planning permission – unless somebody complains.

getting planning permission

It is not illegal to use a property without the relevant planning permission. You cannot be fined unless you have been given 28 days' notice by the local authority to stop the particular 'use'. So if, for example, you use your home as bed and breakfast accommodation which may require planning permission, no fine or other penalty can be imposed by the planning authority until you have been served with an enforcement notice.

The application forms for planning permission for change of use have to be filled in in much the same way as you would if you wanted to make some structural alteration to the property, such as adding an extension. No plans are needed other than a location plan which shows where your house is.

In all cases which involve working from home it is worthwhile first discussing the problems with the local planning authority, and getting advice on whatever permission is needed and the best method of making an application. If the proposal requires planning permission, do not assume that this would automatically be refused.

Many local authorities grant conditional permission on a personal basis, to enable an individual to carry out a limited amount of work from home, but the permission would not extend to sharing part of the accommodation with colleagues or friends to carry out jointly certain types of work on the property.

A planning permission for a change of use of one room to an office, or storage space, or workshop, may involve a change in your rates. You will not be entitled in full to the concessionary rates poundage which applies to the residential part of your property. There is a sliding scale for so-called mixed hereditaments, according to how much is the residential and how much the commercial use. Where the residential element is over 50% of the rateable value, the poundage is about half-way between domestic and commercial.

Also, there is a risk that part of your property may be subject to capital gains tax if you sell it while part of it is used for commercial purposes.

rates

Rates are a tax raised by the local authority to provide money towards financing local services. Revenue from rates contributes to the cost of housing, schooling, the police, provision and maintenance of streets and roads, street lighting, refuse collection, libraries, swimming pools and other public amenities.

how rates are calculated

The rates you pay depend on the rateable value of your property. This is calculated and determined by the Inland Revenue, whose local officials are valuation officers, also known as district valuers (valuation assessors in Scotland). The amount which is to be paid on a property is its rateable value multiplied by the rates poundage, which is fixed annually by the local authority.

rateable value

The valuation officer gives a gross value to the property, based on an estimate of a rent which could have been charged to a tenant for the property if it had been on the market in 1972 (even if built later), the hypothetical landlord being responsible for the cost of repairs and insurance.

Until the next revaluation, the value will continue to be based on rents payable in the year before the last revaluation which was 1973 in England and Wales, 1978 in Scotland.

From the gross value, a notional amount for repairs and insurance is deducted, to arrive at the rateable value, namely:

gross value	rateable value
£65 or less	55% of gross value
£66 to £128	£36 plus seven-tenths of amount by which gross value exceeds £65
£129 to £316	£80 plus five-sixths of amount by which gross value exceeds £128
£317 to £332	gross value less £80
£333 to £430	£250 plus four-fifths of amount by which gross value exceeds £330
over £430	£330 plus five-sixths of amount by which gross value exceeds £430

Before the last revaluation in 1973, the valuation officer collected together all the available open-market rents for residential properties in his particular area. He was thus able to build up a picture of approximately how much per square foot/metre each type of dwelling could be let at that time. For example, modern houses would generally achieve a slightly higher rent than pre-first world war houses. Equally, the location is important: houses situated in 'better' locations would be valued at a higher rate per square foot. The valuation officer, therefore, could create bands of houses in different localities and place a reasonable value per square foot on similar types of accommodation. A 'tone of the list' was thereby created to ensure that there is fairness and uniformity between different classes of dwellings and that similar properties have similar rating assessments. The tone of the list is a key consideration in any appeal against a rateable value assessment.

To produce a basic value per square foot/metre, the valuation officer measures dwellings in one of two ways. It does not matter which method he adopts, because he will use the same method for every dwelling in his area. But it is important if you are appealing against your assessment to know the method he has adopted, so that you can check his measurements for yourself. The two methods are:
• based on external measurements of the house (the simplest method because it usually involves only two measurements)

- based on the internal floor area. This involves measuring every habitable room, including bathroom (but not circulation areas such as hallway or corridors or w.c.'s); the full floor area of rooms is measured, including space taken up by any wardrobes or cupboards which could be dismantled by an outgoing occupier.

A garage of up to 25 square metres, whether it is part of the house, attached to it, or free-standing, is rated at the same domestic rate as the house, so long as it is on the same plot of property as that on which your home is, unless the garage is used for commercial purposes such as keeping a taxi.

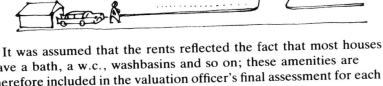

It was assumed that the rents reflected the fact that most houses have a bath, a w.c., washbasins and so on; these amenities are therefore included in the valuation officer's final assessment for each residential property. If there are other amenities, such as an additional w.c., or an en-suite bathroom, or a swimming pool, an additional value will normally be attributed to them.

Central heating was also subject to an additional figure, because at the time of the last revaluation it was not as common as it is today and many of the open-market rents analysed were on properties that did not have central heating. (Since 1974, central heating will not be valued for rating purposes, but if the property is a brand-new one and has central heating, it will be additionally valued. Night storage heaters, or electrically operated oil-filled radiators do not count as central heating for an increase in rateable value, because they are removable and not considered a fixture of the property.)

You can find the individual figures per square foot in your area, and for each of the relevant extra amenities, by contacting the local valuation officer. The telephone number is listed under Inland Revenue Valuation Office (in Scotland, under Regional Council: assessor and electoral registration).

rates poundage

The amount you are asked to pay per £1 of the rateable value will depend on the amount of revenue the local authority wants to raise. Once they know their total budget commitment for the coming financial year, they divide it by the rateable value of all the properties within their district to arrive at the amount of money they need to raise per £1 of rateable value.

In most areas, there are three levels of money allocated to the rateable value of various premises: residential properties, commercial properties, and buildings known as mixed hereditaments (a combination of commercial and residential use). The assessment on a residential property is lower than that for a commercial building; central government pays the difference.

improvements

The rateable value of a house or flat is not affected by who lives in it. When it is sold, the rateable value does not change. But improvements and additions to the house may increase the gross value. Some improvements carried out since 1974 will not affect the value until the next revaluation, namely the installation of central heating and improvements which would raise the gross value by not more than £30.

building alterations

If a property is being so extensively altered that, during the period of alterations, the property is partly or completely uninhabitable, it is possible to get the rateable value reduced to a nominal £1. An application for this should be made as early as possible. Provided the application to the valuation officer is made while the work is being carried out, the reduction would start from when the work started or the beginning of the rate period, whichever is the later. The decision of the valuation officer cannot be backdated to before the date on which the work started.

As soon as the work is completed and the property is again habitable, the rating assessment would again be revalued.

Even if a property remains habitable but is so to a lesser extent (for example, two rooms become unusable), it may be possible to have the value attributed to those rooms taken off the assessment – and, in addition, a building disturbance allowance may be given to reflect the nuisance suffered while the works are continuing.

If an alteration to your property results in the area of accommodation increasing or decreasing, or the use of the property changing from or to residential, your rates assessment should be changed. There is no penalty for not notifying the valuation officer of alterations to your property; he may, in any case, be informed by the local authority if, for example, you have applied for planning permission.

appealing against a rates valuation

An appeal could be made against a new proposal put forward by a valuation officer, or against an existing assessment if you have reason to believe that the gross value is higher than it should be.

appeal against proposal

The valuation officer puts forward a proposal for the assessment of the rateable value either because the property has been extended (for example, an extra room or a garage added, or a loft converted), or because the property itself is a new one which has not been rated before.

If the proposal is based on what you consider to be an incorrect floor area, you should check the measurements and be prepared for the valuation officer to do so, too.

The owner or occupier of the property has 28 days from the date of the proposal to object to it. But, in the meantime, he must not withhold payment. To object, all you have to do is to write a short letter in which you state your reasons. Such an objection is acknowledged, but very little is likely to happen straightaway.

If you do not respond within 28 days, the valuation officer's proposals will be accepted and your rates bill based on it. But you can then appeal against it as an existing assessment.

appeals against an existing assessment

You can appeal against your rates assessment if you become aware that a higher rateable value is put on your property than on a similar property in the same area.

The gross values for all homes in an area are shown on the

valuation list which is kept at the local authority offices. (In Scotland, the valuation roll is kept at Assessors' offices, regional council offices, and in some libraries.) Have a look around in your area for similar homes to yours, and note the exact addresses. Then you can ask to see the appropriate part of the list, and copy down any details you like. Look up the gross values of similar properties to your own in the valuation list to see how they compare with yours.

You can also make an appeal to get your valuation decreased where your property is adversely affected by some change in the immediate environment, such as:

* a building being constructed, which overlooks a (formerly) private garden
* undesirable use of neighbouring land (such as construction of a garage or a car park)
* the immediate vicinity having deteriorated as a result of decline of that section of the town
* the level of traffic on the road having increased as a result of traffic management decisions, such as change of a one-way system
* substantial building operations taking place on adjoining land or land very close to your property (for example, tower cranes being erected which swing over the top of your property, or dust and noise of large-scale building works).

other reasons for an appeal

When there has been a change in the way you use your premises which should result in a reduction in your rates bill and you have informed the local authority, you can appeal if your assessment is not changed.

An appeal against the current assessment could be made where a building was rated as commercial *and* residential accommodation and then the whole property is turned over to a residential use; for example, where two or three rooms had been rated as offices, and then a business that had been run from them ceases and the whole property changes back to residential use.

reasons for not appealing

Although alterations of less than £30 gross value are ignored by the valuation officer, and also central heating installed on existing properties since 1974, these items are taken into account by the valuation officer if an appeal is lodged.

For example, if an assessment is £400 gross value and central heating installed in 1977 is worth, say, £50 gross value, a reduction of more than £50 would need to be obtained for the assessment to be actually reduced. If the disability on which the appeal is based is serious, for example building works next-door resulting in loss of privacy, and the valuation officer allows a reduction of £300, the assessment would only go down by £250 gross value.

the procedure for a rates appeal

You do not have to use a specific form, but it is easier if you do. Contact the local valuation officer and ask for a copy of 'proposal for alteration of valuation list'. Fill in your name (and that of the owner if you are a tenant) sign the form and state whether you are the owner/occupier or leaseholder of the property, or landlord's agent.

In the centre of the form is a space for the reasons why you wish to appeal against the existing assessment. Do not go into great detail. There is a time gap between the appeal and when the decision is made on it. By then, your original arguments may require adjustment, so do not box yourself in by being too precise. Simply say that you believe that the existing assessment is incorrect and excessive (that your property is 'not in line with the tone of the list' would indicate that you are aware of somebody else having a similar property who seems to be paying less rates than you are).

You should ask for a reduction, but you do not have to say what you think the valuation should be. If you do mention a figure, aim on the low side because the local valuation court cannot reduce your valuation below the figure you state.

what happens next

Do not expect any immediate action. Your form will be acknowledged within 28 days and then the valuation officer will probably notify you formally that he does not agree. This is a routine response and does not necessarily mean that you will not succeed.

Someone from the valuation office may visit you to check measurements and see if you have made improvements which could affect the valuation. After this, the valuation officer may agree with your proposal, and reduce your valuation. This is most likely to happen if a mistake is discovered, or if your case is a very straightforward one.

After about 9 to 12 months, if an agreement has not been reached and the proposal is not withdrawn, the matter will be referred to the local valuation court. The court will notify you of the date of the hearing. Prepare your case as fully as possible – the more details you can give the court the better. If your appeal is because of a disturbance such as noise or smells, keep a record of when you notice the problem over a period of a few weeks. Get neighbours to help as well, especially if they are also trying to get their valuation reduced.

The valuation court is a semi-formal panel who will listen to your reasons for appealing, and to the valuation officer's argument in support of the existing or proposed assessment.

The panel may come to a decision there and then, or may write to you later. You can ask for the reasons for their decision.

In practice, normally a meeting takes place with the valuation officer before the hearing of the valuation court to see if an agreement can be reached. This is the time for any practical negotiations to take place. You will get an idea of how much room for manoeuvre the valuation officer may have. He may offer you a reduction because an error was made in assessing the rateable value – or he may advise you that there is no chance of a reduction.

if successful
If you win, it might be worth applying for the reduction to be backdated.

If your appeal for a lower valuation is successful, any increase due to improvements will be set against any reductions you might win. The valuation officer may have advised you to withdraw your proposals because you have made improvements to your home and not had the valuation increased.

water charges

The water charges, payable to the regional water authority or the local water company, are based on the rateable value of your home. If this is reduced following an appeal, part of the water charges should also be reduced.

taking action

Hundreds of people, every week, up and down the country, state their case before the local valuation courts. It is not something to be frightened of. The *Which?* money-saving kit *Find out if and how you can reduce your rates bill* includes a step-by-step guide to the appeal procedure.

some relevant Which? reports

Burst pipes *Which?* December 1983
Buying a new house *Which?* July 1984
Complaining *Which?* January 1984
Condensation *Handyman Which?* May 1981
Damp *Handyman Which?* May 1979
Double glazing *Handyman Which?* August 1982
Electrical fittings *Handyman Which?* November 1982
Electric plugs *Which?* October 1983
Electrical wiring *Which?* February 1984
Extending your home *Which?* May 1983
Flooring *Which?* August 1982
  – **wood** *Handyman Which?* August 1981
Home improvement grants *Which?* February 1984
House contents insurance *Which?* February 1984
House exteriors *Which?* April 1984
House surveys *Which?* May 1983
Lead *Which?* August 1984
Local government services *Which?* January 1984
Loft insulation *Handyman Which?* May 1980
Loft ladders *Which?* February 1983
Painting house exteriors *Which?* April 1984
Paints
  – **emulsion** *Which?* January 1983
  – **gloss** *Handyman Which?* May 1982
  – **outdoor gloss** *Which?* April 1984
Plastering *Handyman Which?* November 1979
Plumbers *Which?* September 1983

Plumbing made easy *Which?* May 1982
Professional advisers *Which?* July 1983
Rates *Which?* March 1983
 – paying less *Which?* March 1984
Rate rebates and investment income *Which?* March 1984
Roof repairs *Which?* March 1984
Rot, wet and dry *Handyman Which?* May 1979
Thatched roof repairs *Which?* March 1984
Securing your home *Handyman Which?* February 1981
Surveyors *Which?* May 1983
Trees *Handyman Which?* August 1979
Walls, knocking holes in *Which?* April 1983
Weeds: killing *Which?* May 1983
Wiring, household *Which?* February 1984
Wood finishes, exterior *Which?* April 1984
Working off the ground *Which?* May 1984

some relevant CA books
Dealing with household emergencies
Earning money at home
Living with stress
Securing your home
Starting your own business
The legal side of buying a house
The Which? book of do-it-yourself
The Which? book of home improvements and extensions
The Which? book of insurance
Which? way to buy, sell and move house

index

abandoned cars, 91
adopted roads, 91 *et seq*
adverse possession, 11
air bricks, 60
Aluminium Window Assn, 67
animals, 21, 25, 27 *et seq*, 83
Arboricultural Association, 19
arboriculturist, 19
architect, 64, 76, 83, 101, 102, 104
– and fees, 108
asbestos, 40, 88
Association of Noise Consultants, 67

balls, 23, 26
basement, 62, 63
bathroom, 44, 61, 62, 73, 96, 97, 103,
  125, 130
bedroom, 61, 96
bond, new roads, 92
bonfires, 23 *et seq*, 89
Botanical Identification, 17
boundary, 6, 9 *et seq*, 24, 42, 85
– and location, 9
– and ownership, 9
– and trees, 16, 18
– and walls, 12 *et seq*
branches, overhanging, 18
Brick Development Assn, 67
brickwork, 54, 56, 57, 58, 59, 61, 63
British Board of Agrement, 67
British Chemical Damp Course Assn, 64,
  67
British Decorators Federation, 67
Building Research Advisory Service,
  68
British Standards, trees, 20
British Wood Preserving Assn, 64, 68
building works, 5 *et seq*
– and neighbours, 34
builder's negligence, 40
builder's radio, 39
builders, 70 *et seq*
– and codes of practice, 80
– and complaints, 79
– and delays, 78
– and extra time, 74 *et seq*

– and grants, 103
– and insurance, 81
– and new roads, 92
– and payment, 77
– and price, 72
– and redress, 80
– and schedule of works, 77
– and specification, 72
– and standard of work, 75
– and tender, 72
– and time, 74 *et seq*
Building Employers Confederation, 71
Building Regulations, 76, 87, 105 *et seq*
– and application fee, 107
– and contravention, 109 *et seq*
– and fees, 107 *et seq*
– and grants, 100, 102
– and notice of commencement, 109
– and plan inspection fee, 108
– and Scotland, 110
burglars, 39, 81
by-laws, 23, 83, 88

capital gains tax, 127
car, 19
– abandoned, 91
– and insurance, 83
– and parking, 90 *et seq*, 134
cavity walls, 59
central heating, 63, 130, 131
cesspool, 94 *et seq*
Chartered Institute of Arbitrators, 68
Chartered surveyor, *see* surveyor
children, 21, 23, 26, 123
chimney, 23, 52 *et seq*
chimney stack, 52, 54
citizens advice bureau, 32, 33, 47, 77
clay soil, 17
Clean Air Act, 23, 24, 89
code of practice, 80
condensation, 61 *et seq*
conservation areas, 34, 35, 121 *et seq*
contract and builder, 71, 74 *et seq*, 77, 78
Control of Pollution Act, 23, 29, 31, 39
councillors, 36, 87
court, 18, 21, 27, 46, 49, 90

damage by trees, 17, 81, 84
damp, 47, 54, 57, 61, 62, 84, 105
damp-proof course, 26, 59 *et seq*, 73, 98
defects, 50 *et seq*, 66
delays and builder, 78
development, 113 *et seq*
– and listed buildings, 122
– and planning permission, 123 *et seq*
– permitted, 113 *et seq*
disabled, 97
– and grants, 99, 101, 103
– and insulation, 100
– and planning permission, 117
district councils, 86
district surveyor, 7, 104, 111, 112
– and fees, 112
district valuer, 128 *et seq*
ditch, 10, 11
dog and trespassers, 25
double-glazing, 57
downpipes, 8, 55, 56
– and grants, 98
drainage, 94
– and Building Regulations, 105
drains, tree damage, 17, 44, 65
Draught Proofing Advisory Assn Ltd, 68
drives, 82
– and insurance, 93
dry rot, 41, 50, 60, 63 *et seq*, 66
dust, 40 *et seq*, 134

earning money from home, 123 *et seq*
elderly and insulation, 100
– and loans, 100, 123
electrician, 64, 73, 75, 77, 79
enforcement notice, 119 *et seq*
– and listed building, 121
– and planning permission, 126
empty rates, 131
entry, right of, 13
Environment, Dept of, 33, 87
environmental health dept, 29, 40, 47, 87
– and grants, 97
– and repair, 46
estimate, 65, 72, 76, 77, 78
– and grants, 103
eviction, 44 *et seq*
– protection from, 48
exclusions and insurance, 81 *et seq*
expert and rot, 64, 65 *et seq*
– and complaints, 67
– and insurance, 83

extensions, 71, 102, 105, 108, 114, 118, 126
External Wall Insulation Assn, 68

Faculty of Architects and Surveyors, 68
Federation of Master Builders, 70
fees, Building Regulations, 107 *et seq*
– and planning permission, 117
Felt Roofing Contractors' Advisory
  Board, 68
fence, 9, 12 *et seq*, 81, 82
– and animals, 28
– and planning permission, 114
Fencing Contractors' Assn, 68
fire, 81, 98
– and Building Regulations, 105, 106
– and Inner London, 112
fireplace, 89
flashing, metal, 52 *et seq*
flat, 9, 91
– and grants, 97
– and planning permission, 113, 125
– and service charges, 91, 98
flat roof, 54 *et seq*, 116
floors, 44, 47
– and rot, 62
fly-posting, 26
footpaths, 90
Forestry Commission Research Station,
  19
foundations, 17, 19
– and Building Regulations, 108
– and grants, 98
freeholder and grants, 100, 101
fruit, 18
fungi, 41

gates, 81, 82
– and planning permission, 114
garages, 40, 81, 91, 117, 124, 130, 133, 134
garden, 9, 24, 29, 114
– and rubbish, 24, 88
– and shed, 114
gales, 18, 71, 81, 84, 89, 117
Glass and Glazing Federation, 68
grants, 96 *et seq*
– applying for, 101 *et seq*
– Building Regulations, 100
– disabled, 97, 99, 101, 103
– estimate, 103
– housing action area, 97
– improvement, 96 *et seq*, 107

– insulation, 100
– intermediate, 96, 97 *et seq*, 107
– loans, 100
– multiple occupation, 99
– planning permission, 100
– repairs, 96, 98 *et seq*
– special, 96, 99
– traffic noise, 33, 65, 76
Greater London Council, 86, 110
greenhouse, 84, 114
gross value, rates, 129
guarantee, 70, 71, 77, 92
Guaranteed Treatment Protection Trust
  Ltd, 64, 68
guests, paying, 125
guttering, 8, 26, 44, 50, 54, 55 *et seq*
– and grants, 98
– and insurance, 84

harassment, protection from, 48, 49
Health and Social Security, Dept of, 99
Heating and Ventilating Contractors
  Assn, 68
hedge, 9, 10, 12 *et seq*, 21, 81, 82
– and trimming, 14
highways, 90, 91
Highways Acts, 89, 92
home, earning money from, 123 *et seq*
house, terraced, 6, 9, 114
housing action area, 97
Housing Acts, 47, 96, 102
housing aid centre, 47

Incorporated Assn of Architects and
  Surveyors, 68
injunction, 7, 30
Inner London, *see* London
Institute of Plumbing, 69
insulation and asbestos, 40
– and Building Regulations, 105
– and condensation, 61
– and grants, 100
– and loft, 100
– and roof, 61
insurance, 8, 17, 19, 27, 65
– and builder, 70, 71
– and claiming, 81 *et seq*
– and contents, 83
– and exclusions, 82
– and household contents, 84
– and legal expenses, 85
– and liability, 83

– and personal liability, 27, 84
– and public liability, 19
– and rates, 129
– and wear and tear, 84

kitchen, 61, 62, 74, 94

ladder, 26, 56
land certificate, 9
Land Compensation Code, 33
Land Registry, 9, 16
landlord, 44 *et seq*
– and grants, 96 *et seq*
– and insurance, 83
– and rates, 128, 135
lead, 41
lead roof, 53, 55
lease, 9, 14, 16, 44 *et seq*
leaseholder, 99, 101, 135
legal expenses insurance, 85
light, 18, 36
– prescriptive right to, 18, 37, 116
listed buildings, 121
local authority, 86 *et seq*
loft, 60 *et seq*
– insulation, 100
– and planning permission, 114
– and rates, 133
London Housing Aid Centre, 48, 49
London, Inner, 6
– and Building Regulations, 110, 111, 112
– and district surveyor, 104
– and grants, 97, 98, 99

magistrates' court, 29, 30 *et seq*, 47, 88
Metal Roofing Contractors' Ass Assn, 69
mixed hereditaments, 127, 131
multiple occupation, 7, 99, 113
– and planning permission, 125

National Assn of Plumbing Heating and
  Mechanical Services Contractors, 69
National Cavity Insulation Assn, 69
National Federation of Roofing
  Contractors, 69
National Home Enlargement Bureau, 71
National Self-Builders Assn, 69
National Society for Clean Air, 24, 89
negligence, 8, 18, 27, 40, 66, 79
neighbours, 5 *et seq*
– and building works, 34
– and development, 124, 126

– and disrepair, 7
– and nuisance, 24 *et seq*, 85
– and planning applications, 34, 115, 117
– and trees, 18
noise, 6, 23 *et seq*, 35
– and building work, 39, 78, 85
– and neighbours, 29 *et seq*, 39
– and rates, 136
– and traffic, 33
nuisance, 23 *et seq*
– abatement order, 24
– and neighbours, 24 *et seq*, 85
– and neighbours building works, 39
– and noise, 29, 39
– and sewers, 94
– statutory, 23, 47

Office of Fair Trading, 76 *et seq*
owner, 5, 9 *et seq*
– and liability, 45

paint, lead in, 41
paraffin heater, 61
parked cars, 90 *et seq*
party fence, 12
party walls, 5 *et seq*
pavement, 20, 90, 91
paying guests, 125
payment to builder, 77
pensioners and loans, 100
– and insulation, 100
personal liability insurance, 27, 84
pipes, 44, 66, 67, 82, 94
– and grants, 100
planning permission, 14, 35, 38, 76, 86, 87, 113 *et seq*
– application, 34, 116, 117, 126
– and development, 113 *et seq*, 123 *et seq*
– and disabled, 117
– and drawings, 117
– and fees, 117
– and fences and gates, 115
– and listed buildings, 121
– and penalties, 118 *et seq*
– and professional use, 125
– and rates, 132
– and refusal, 118
– and time taken, 118
– and trees and walls, 115
plumbing, 29, 44, 60, 61, 63, 65, 75, 77, 79
pointing, 52, 58
police, 25, 28, 32, 89, 90, 91, 128

porch, 108, 114, 122
preservation notice, 122
preservation order, trees, 21 *et seq*
Princes Risborough Laboratory, 68
privacy, 36
protection from eviction, 48 *et seq*
public enquiry, 120

quotation, builders', 72, 74, 75, 76, 78
– and grant, 101

rates, 128 *et seq*
– appeal against, 133 *et seq*
– empty, 131
– gross value, 129 *et seq*
– poundage, 131
– rateable value, 128 *et seq*
– reduction, 33
refuse disposal, 86, 87 *et seq*
regulated tenancy, 44
Rent Acts, 44, 102
rent arrears, 46
repairs, 12 *et seq*, 44 *et seq*
– responsibility for, 44
restrictive covenants, 14
rewiring, 79, 98
right to light, 37, 116
right to view, 38
right of way, 10
rights, acquiring, 11
– prescriptive, 13
river, 11 *et seq*, 38
roads, 86, 90, 128
– adopted/unadopted, 91
– new, 92
roof, 44, 47, 50, 51, 53 *et seq*, 65
– flat, 54, 116
– and grants, 98
– and insurance, 83, 84
– and planning permission, 117
– pitched, 60
– and repairs, 71
– working on, 56
– and woodworm, 62, 63, 67
rot, wet and dry, 63 *et seq*
Royal Forestry Society, 19
Royal Institute of British Architects, 69, 74
Royal Institution of Chartered Surveyors, 69, 74
Royal Town Planning Institute, 118
rubbish skip, 41, 87 *et seq*

scaffolding, 39, 90
schedule of works, 72
Scotland, 29, 30, 32, 86, 110
Scottish Decorators Assn, 69
Scottish Office, 33
septic tanks, 94
service charges, 91
sewer, private, 94, 105
– public, 94
sewerage, 93 *et seq*
SHAC, 48, 49
shed, 40, 114
sheriff court, 29, 30
skip, 41, 87, 88 *et seq*, 90
skirting and rot, 62
slates, 54, 60, 71, 83, 84
smoke, 23 *et seq*
smoke control areas, 89
specialists, building, 67 *et seq*
specification and builder, 72
soil, clay, 17
solicitor, 32, 83, 85
stairway, 44
statutory nuisance, 29, 47
statutory tenant, 44, 102
stop notice, 120 *et seq*
storm, 17, 71, 81, 84
street, 14, 91, 117, 121
– cleaning, 90
– trees in, 19, 20
subcontractor, 72, 75 *et seq*, 77, 79
subsidence and insurance, 82
surveyor, 17, 20, 42, 65, 66 *et seq*, 76, 83,
    101, 102, 103, 104

T-marks, 9
tax, capital gains, 127
television aerial, 82
tenancy, regulated, 44
– statutory, 102
– tenant, 44 *et seq*
– and grants, 96 *et seq*, 99, 101
– and insurance, 83
– and rates, 128, 135
– and repairs, 44 *et seq*
– and roads, 93
tender, builder's, 72, 78
terraced house, 6, 9, 114
Thermal Insulating Contractors' Assn, 69
tiles, 53, 54
– and insurance, 84
– and roof, 54, 60, 71

timber, 41, 50, 54, 55, 63, 66, 98
Timber Research and Development Assn,
    69
timber specialist, 65
title deeds, 9, 12, 14, 44
Town and Country Planning Act, 119
tree care specialist, 19
tree surgeon, 19
trees, 16 *et seq*, 25
– and insurance, 83, 84
– and planning permission, 115
– and preservation order, 21 *et seq*
– and roots, 16 *et seq*
trespass, 13, 25 *et seq*
– and animals, 28

valuation court, 135 *et seq*
valuation officer, 128 *et seq*
value added tax, 103, 108, 109
variations, builders, 72
vehicle, abandoned, 91
– and insurance, 83
– parked, 90 *et seq*, 134
– selling, 124
ventilation, 60, 61, 63, 105
vibration, 23, 41 *et seq*
view, right to, 38

Wales, 86, 110, 114
– and rates, 128
walls, 44, 50, 81
– party, 5 *et seq*, 13
– and grants, 98, 105, 108
– and planning permission, 114, 117
water, 11 *et seq*, 59, 60, 82
– and bill, 95
– and charges, 137
– and grants, 102
– and hot and cold, 97
– and rights over, 12, 57, 58, 61
water authority, 94, 137
w.c., 44, 62, 96, 97, 102, 125, 130
wet rot, 63
windows, 27, 37, 38, 40, 47, 57, 74, 117
– and condensation, 62
– and grants, 98
– and rot, 63
window sill, 57 *et seq*
woodworm, 62, 66
work from home, 123 *et seq*
workmanship, substandard, 79